KU-298-129

CHILTERNS WALKS FOR MOTORISTS

Southern Area

Warne Gerrard Guides for Walkers

Walks for Motorists Series

CHESHIRE WALKS

CHILTERNS WALKS
          Northern
          Southern

COTSWOLDS WALKS
          Northern
          Southern

JERSEY WALKS

LAKE DISTRICT WALKS
          Central
          Northern
          Western

LONDON COUNTRYSIDE WALKS
          North West
          North East
          South West
          South East

GREEN LONDON WALKS
          (both circular and cross country)

MIDLAND WALKS

NORTH YORK MOORS WALKS
          North and East
          West and South

PEAK DISTRICT WALKS

PENDLESIDE AND BRONTE COUNTRY WALKS

SNOWDONIA WALKS
          Northern

YORKSHIRE DALES WALKS

FURTHER DALES WALKS

Long Distance and Cross Country Walks

WALKING THE PENNINE WAY

RAMBLES IN THE DALES

CHILTERNS

WALKS FOR MOTORISTS
SOUTHERN AREA

Nicholas Moon

30 Sketch maps by Ray Martin
6 Photographs by Don Gresswell

BUCKS COUNTY LIBRARY

W/   WEA   1863/79

∠450·91
MOO

FREDERICK WARNE

Published by
Frederick Warne (Publishers) Ltd.
40 Bedford Square,
London WC1B 3HE

© Frederick Warne (Publishers) Ltd 1979

The photograph on the front cover
is a view of Fingest; that on
the back cover is of Stonor House

Acknowledgements

My particular thanks go to Don Gresswell for his invaluable
help, both in practical matters and in advice and encourage-
ment. My thanks also go to my colleagues in the Chiltern
Society (Rights of Way Group), Oxford Fieldpaths Society and
Ramblers Association, for their help in the resolution of path
problems; and to Mick Fryer for his tales of old Bucks.

Publishers' Note

While every care has been taken in the compilation of this
book, the publishers cannot accept responsibility for any
inaccuracies. But things may have changed since the book
was published: paths are sometimes diverted, a concrete
bridge may replace a wooden one, stiles disappear. Please let
the publishers know if you discover anything like this on your
way.
   The length of each walk in this book is given in miles and
kilometres, but within the text Imperial measurements are
quoted. It is useful to bear the following approximations in
mind:
5 miles = 8 kilometes, $\frac{1}{2}$ mile = 804 metres, 1 metre = 39.4
inches.

ISBN 0 7232 2145 6

Phototypeset by Tradespools Ltd, Frome, Somerset
Printed by Galava Printing Co. Ltd., Nelson, Lancashire

Contents

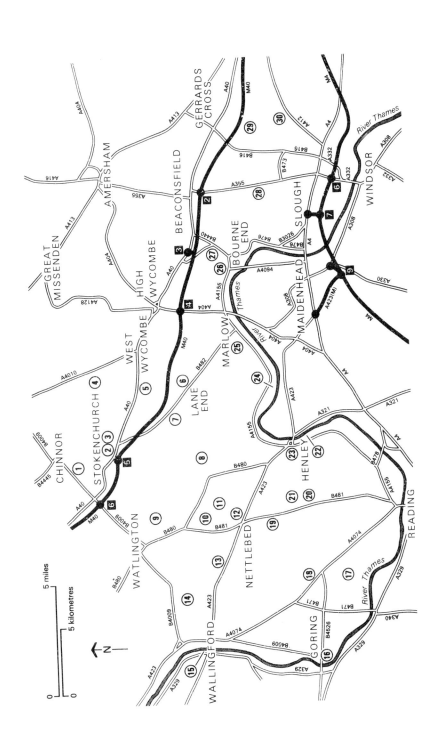

Introduction

The Chiltern Hills form an approximately 500-square-mile triangle to the west and north-west of London bounded by the River Thames to the south, the Lower Icknield Way to the north-west and the River Colne and the M1 to the east. Being the nearest outstanding countryside outside London, the Chilterns have been subject to considerable pressures for development, motorways and recreational activities. Despite substantial development over the years, the western and northern parts of the Chilterns have remained completely rural in character, while the south-eastern part has been protected thanks to the Green Belt policy which preserves areas of countryside between the large commuter belt communities. In 1965 the Chiltern Society was set up to promote a sense of identity for the area and minimize further erosion of its rural status. The Area of Outstanding Natural Beauty was also created at this time.

A cross-section of the many varying types of Chiltern countryside can be seen in the walks here described. On the north-western edge of the area covered is the steep and lofty Chiltern escarpment, with its mixture of woodland and open downland, often degenerating into scrub, dropping down to the Oxfordshire Plain. On the southern edge is the Thames Valley, which the river has carved through the hills, and where the beauty of the riverside is complemented by scenic backdrops. The interior also has much to offer the walker. The western Bucks and northern Oxfordshire Chilterns have landscape predominantly consisting of steep ridges and deep, generally dry valleys with an irregular mixture of woodland, arable and livestock farming presenting a constantly changing scene to the walker. The southern Oxfordshire Chilterns have a less pronounced, more rolling and lush landscape which is generally heavily wooded and very peaceful. East of the Wye Valley, however, where the south-east Chilterns plateau drops gradually into the Colne and Thames valleys, the countryside is more artificial with large areas of parkland and woodland and comparatively little agriculture. This area, nevertheless, offers some pleasant walks, particularly in spring and autumn.

All the walks described here follow public rights of way, use permissive paths across land owned by public bodies or cross public open space. As the majority of walks cross land used for economic purposes such as agriculture, forestry or the rearing of game, walkers are urged to follow the Country Code at all times:

Keep dogs under proper control.
Guard against fire risk.
Keep to the paths across farmland.

7

Fasten all gates.
Go carefully on country roads.
Leave no litter.
Respect the life of the countryside.
Safeguard water supplies.
Avoid damaging fences, hedges and walls.
Protect wild life, wild plants and trees.

Observing these rules helps prevent financial loss to landowners and damage to the environment, as well as the all-too-frequent and often justified bad feeling towards walkers in the countryside.

The Ordnance Survey map references indicating the starting places of the walks consist of six figures in groups of three, each group locating imaginary vertical and horizontal lines, the intersection of which indicates the place required on the map. The first two figures refer to one of the vertical grid lines identified by a number to be found along the top and bottom of the map. The third figure represents tenths of the distance between that line and the next one to the right. Similarly the next two figures locate one of the horizontal grid lines, and the final one represents tenths of the distance between it and the next one above. The locality required is within 50 metres of the intersection of these two imaginary lines.

As for equipment, readers are advised that where mud warnings are given, the walks are those on which mud remains in dry weather. At other times, all walks are subject to some mud. In any event proper walking boots are to be recommended at all times. The nature of the countryside makes many Chiltern paths prone to overgrowth, particularly in summer. To avoid resultant discomfort to walkers, protective clothing is advisable, particularly where specific warnings are given.

On timing the walks, at least one hour should be reckoned for every two miles, as the hilly country and frequency of stiles and gates inevitably slow you down. The maps provided are designed to help you find the route without difficulty, but the road network is in diagrammatic form and non-relevant woodland is often simplified or omitted. For details of Amenity Society maps, for example the Chiltern Society Footpath Maps, please phone or write to Mrs Howkins, Spindle Cottage, Quickmoor Lane, Chipperfield, Herts. (Kings Langley 65677).

Walk 1 Crowell

$6\frac{1}{4}$ miles (10 km)

Start: Crowell village green; O S map ref. 744997
Stout footwear is advised; in wet weather wellingtons may be required.

Crowell, a small hamlet below the escarpment sandwiched between two larger neighbours, Chinnor and Kingston Blount, has managed to preserve its identity and its status as an independent parish despite all apparent odds. Believed to be of Anglo-Saxon origin, its name meaning 'Crow's well', the parish is of some historical interest. Its church, although largely rebuilt in 1878, preserves some of the original twelfth-century building. The Catherine Wheel is alleged to have had John Bunyan as a guest. The sixteenth-century farmhouse, Ellwood House, on the other side of the B4009 was the birthplace of Thomas Ellwood, a Quaker and a friend of John Milton. He rented the cottage at Chalfont St Giles for Milton and inspired the poet to write 'Paradise Regained'.

The walk, which follows ancient and largely disused roadways for much of its length, takes in escarpment beechwoods, the picturesque village of Aston Rowant and some extensive views of the escarpment from below.

Crowell, $4\frac{1}{2}$ miles southeast of Thame, may be reached by leaving the M40 at Junction 6 (Lewknor) and following the B4009 towards Chinnor for two miles, turning right onto the village green just past a sign to Crowell Church. Some parking space exists here, but extra space is available on rough lanes leading off the B4009 towards or away from the escarpment.

Starting from Crowell village green in front of the Catherine Wheel, take the lane leading out of the back left-hand corner of the village green towards the escarpment. Soon the hamlet and the macadam surface are left behind and after $\frac{1}{4}$ mile, a hump in the stony road marks the former level crossing on the Watlington Branch Line. Just beyond this to the left is the vast chalk quarry of Chinnor Cement Works. Go straight on and at the far side of the quarry, cross the Upper Icknield Way, an ancient Celtic road named after Boadicea's people, the Iceni. Despite being more dangerous in the past, because of robbers, than the Lower Icknield Way, the upper road was preferred in wet weather as a drier route.

Continue straight on up a hedged lane, the ancient road from Crowell to High Wycombe. On entering a wood, fork left onto a track in the bottom of a deep gulley, which climbs steadily and widens out

9

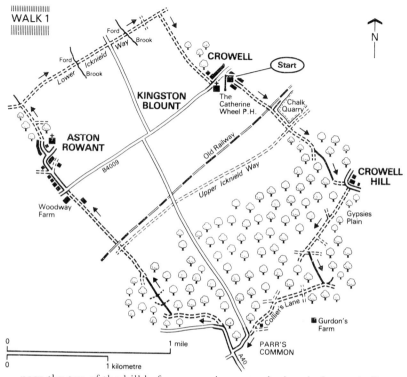

near the top of the hill before emerging onto the bend of a road. On reaching the road, follow it straight on for a few yards and then turn right onto a waymarked path inside the edge of the wood. Follow this path for $\frac{1}{3}$ mile, ignoring all tracks going deeper into the wood. This part of the woodland, which is 800 feet above sea-level, is known by the self explanatory name Gypsies' Plain. Where the edge of the wood turns sharply away to the left, go straight on along the waymarked path. After a further 150 yards, the waymarked path forks half left off the track, crosses another track and shortly becomes flanked by a boundary ridge to the left and a coniferous plantation to the right.

After $\frac{1}{4}$ mile, a sunken track in the bottom of a valley known as Collier's Lane is reached. This is part of the ancient road to Oxford. Turn sharp right onto this track and follow it for over $\frac{1}{2}$ mile, soon joining the edge of the wood. Now follow the track along the inside edge of the wood, ignoring all branching tracks, until you emerge by a double cottage at Parr's Common. Join a farm road here. In a few yards, on reaching a macadam road, bear slightly left. Follow the road to a staggered crossroads with the A40.

Turn right onto the A40 and follow it to a left-hand bend. Here fork right onto a bridleway into the woods (until 1824 this was the course of the main road). After $\frac{1}{4}$ mile, just before a right-hand bend, turn right down a steep gulley. Where the path levels out, ignore a crossing track and descend into a further gulley. Continue straight on now for nearly a mile, leaving the woods behind, crossing the Upper Icknield Way and the old railway and passing the early neo-Tudor Lambert Arms, in trees to the left. On reaching the B4009 by Woodway Farm, cross it and continue straight on along the road into Aston Rowant, ignoring side turnings. Eventually the road bends to the right to Aston Rowant Church, built in the eleventh to fourteenth centuries.

The road to the right leads to the attractive village green, but the walk turns left here into Church Lane, the oldest part of the village. Where the macadam ends, go straight on, ignoring a turning to the right, until you reach a crossing lane, the Lower Icknield Way. Turn right onto this ancient road. On reaching a ford after $\frac{1}{2}$ mile, cross it by way of the stepping-stones on the right-hand side. After another $\frac{1}{4}$ mile, cross a road and go straight on. A further ford at the end of the next field can normally be stepped over on the right-hand side. After two more fields on the right, with the vast modern developments of Chinnor coming into view ahead, turn right onto an unfenced track between fields. Follow this, with Chinnor to the left and Kingston Blount to the right, for $\frac{1}{2}$ mile back to Crowell, where some magnificent chestnut trees greet your approach. On reaching the B4009, cross it, bear slightly left and take a path through a kissing-gate, the churchyard and a lych-gate, back to the village green.

Walk 2
Stokenchurch (North)

$5\frac{3}{4}$ miles (9 km)

Start: King's Arms, Stokenchurch; O S map ref. 760963

Stokenchurch, spread along the A40 London–Oxford road on a ridge-top plateau about a mile from the escarpment and one of the highest major settlements in the Chilterns, has the unfortunate reputation of being 'the ugly duckling' of the Chilterns. This may arise from its role as a centre of the Bucks furniture industry with its consequent factories and timber yards, or from the extent to which it has been developed for housing in recent years. Nevertheless, the village can boast extensive, attractive, well-maintained village greens, where traditionally an annual horse fair used to be held on July 10th and 11th. The twelfth-century church, hidden behind the King's Arms, is of interest despite many renovations, and the King's Arms itself is a long-standing coaching inn on the turnpike road to Oxford. For the walker, however, the chief attraction of Stokenchurch is that it is an ideal centre for exploring some of the finest Chiltern countryside, including the Wormsley Valley, Penley Bottom, Radnage, and the escarpment.

This walk traverses the ridges and bottoms to the north of Stokenchurch, following Colliers Lane, the ancient Oxford road, for some distance and taking in parts of Radnage including Andridge with its fine views.

The starting point for this walk and the next can be reached from the M40 by leaving it at Junction 5 (Stokenchurch) and taking the A40 into the centre of the village. Ample roadside parking is available off the main road, but parking on the grass areas of the village greens is forbidden by local byelaws.

Starting from the King's Arms forecourt at Stokenchurch, head west passing a chemist's shop and a small supermarket, cross a side road and bear half right across a green to the far corner. This was once the village bowling green and the magnificent lime trees on it are the remains of a circle. At the far corner, bear half left by the former village bakehouse into an alleyway between a fence and a hedge leading to a new estate road. Turn right onto this road and follow it round to the left. At the end of the road turn right onto a footpath between the houses to a gate and stile. Beyond the stile follow a hedge downhill, then cross another stile where the hedge swings left and continue to follow it down into a cattle drive leading to a stile. Cross this and bear half left across a steeply rising field. On reaching a hedge, follow it uphill to a stile into a wood. Ignoring a fork to the right, take a winding path downhill through the wood. At the bottom,

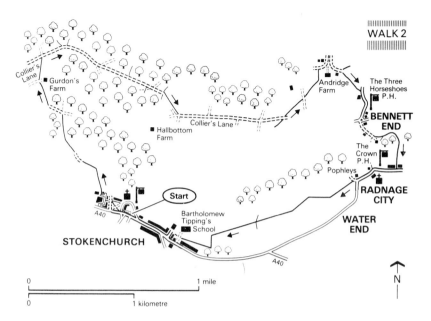

Collier's Lane

Gurdon's Farm

Andridge Farm

The Three Horseshoes P.H.

BENNETT END

Collier's Lane

Hallbottom Farm

The Crown P.H.

Pophleys

RADNAGE CITY

Start

A40

Bartholomew Tipping's School

WATER END

STOKENCHURCH

A40

0   1 mile

0   1 kilometre

N

turn left onto a track. You soon leave the wood by a bridlegate. After about 50 yards turn right following a sporadic hedge uphill to a kissing-gate left of Gurdon's Farm. Go through this and bear half left across a small yard to a stile. Bearing half right here, join a hedge and follow it downhill to some rails beside a New Zealand (barbed wire) gate leading into another wood.

Having climbed through the rails, you come to Collier's Lane, the ancient road from London to Oxford which was replaced by the modern A40 through Stokenchurch. Turn right onto this track which hugs the valley bottom. Ignoring all branching tracks, follow it through the woods for nearly a mile, eventually re-emerging into the open. A few yards beyond this, where the valley meets another in which Hallbottom Farm can be seen to the right, Collier's Lane swings to the left. Continue to follow it along the valley floor for another $\frac{2}{3}$ mile.

On reaching a fenced field to the left, follow the right-hand side of the fence straight on, until coming to a stile. Turn half left here, crossing the stile and the field beyond, heading towards Andridge Farm on the hilltop, to another stile and lane. Cross these and continue straight on across another field, climbing at first gradually, then more steeply, making for an electricity pole in the hedge ahead. On reaching the hedge, turn left along it. At a gap in the corner of the field, first turn round to look at the extensive view across the valley towards Stokenchurch. Now go through the gap and bear right onto a track which takes you through a gate and across a paddock to another

13

gate and stile. Cross the stile, the drive to Andridge Farm and a stile on the other side. Now turn right onto a second drive, which swings left past a bungalow and leads into a field.

Here a magnificent view opens out in front, of Radnage Bottom flanked by Bledlow Ridge to the left and the Radnage Common ridge to the right. In the distance on West Wycombe Hill is St Lawrence's Church, a thirteenth-century church extensively rebuilt in 1763 by Francis Lord le Despencer who added to its tower the golden ball for which it is famous.

Bear half right here onto what is normally a crop break which heads towards some farm buildings with corrugated iron roofs in the valley below. Soon you join a fence and follow it downhill to a road. Some way down the hill, the church which comes into view to the left is that of Radnage, built in the early thirteenth century. Turn right onto the road and follow it downhill into Bennett End. Where the road forks, go right. By an attractive gabled cottage, cross a crossroads and take a bridleway straight on towards a hill. At the foot of a steep slope, where a large house appears ahead, follow the bridleway round to the left. At a fork, go straight on, climbing gradually and curving to the right. When a view opens out to the left, continue straight on between a hedge and a fence, crossing a ladder stile and eventually emerging on a road in grandiose-sounding Radnage City.

Turn right onto the road called City Road and follow it for $\frac{1}{4}$ mile, passing the Crown. When you reach the driveway to Pophleys at a sharp left-hand bend fork right. Where the drive turns right continue straight on, crossing a stile into a hedged path leading to another stile. Having crossed this, bear half left across a field to a stile at the end of a hedge by the furthest right of several holly trees. Turn round to look at the extensive view before continuing straight on over the stile and along a winding grass track across fields towards Stokenchurch. After more than $\frac{1}{2}$ mile, the path becomes enclosed between a hedge and a fence. After a further 200 yards it turns left and follows the perimeter of a school playing field. On reaching a metal kissing-gate, turn left down a school drive to the A40. Turn right and follow the A40 for $\frac{1}{4}$ mile back to your point of departure.

Walk 3   Stokenchurch (South)

5 miles (8 km)

Start: King's Arms, Stokenchurch; O S map ref. 760963 (see Walk 2)

This walk, to the south of Stokenchurch, includes a fine viewpoint at Studdridge Farm, the heathy northern end of Ibstone Common and the secluded Wormsley Valley as well as much fine country in between.

Starting from the King's Arms, Stokenchurch, cross the A40 and keeping right of the Four Horseshoes take the road across the green to Coopers Court Road. Follow this downhill, crossing Slade Road to the tunnel under the M40. At the far end of this, fork right into the drive to Fowler's Farm and cross a stile to the left of a gate into a field, Bear half left across the field to another stile to the left of the farmhouse and a large tree. Turn left over the stile and follow a cattle drive alongside a hedge. It may be necessary at one or two points to go through New Zealand (barbed-wire) gates which are placed across the path to route cattle to the required destination. To avoid inconvenience to the farmer these should be left as they are found. At the end of the cattle drive, the path enters a field and follows the hedge downhill to a stile. Cross the stile and follow the path uphill by a fence through a belt of trees to a stile and gate. Cross this and follow a hedge uphill, possibly having to cross wooden rails at the mouth of a cattle drive half way up, to a pair of stiles at the top. Beyond these, fork half left across a field to the left-hand nearside corner of a group of trees concealing two ponds. Follow the left side of this group to the far end. Then bear half right across the field to a gate on the drive to Studdridge Farm.

Join the drive and follow it past the farmhouse. Where the drive turns left, continue straight on to a stile between two barns. Here a magnificent view opens out towards the distant Thames Valley. Cross the stile and in a few yards go through a gate. Then follow the fence and hedge on the right to a gate in a crossing hedge. Go through this and follow a grassy track beside a hedge and line of trees until the track swings to the left. Here some wooden rails hidden behind a tree lead into an area of scrubland. Turn right, crossing these rails, then bear half left through the thicket to some more rails leading into a field. Cross these, turn right and follow the edge of a wood downhill to a 'stile' in the corner of the field. Enter clear-felled woodland here and a few yards in, at a T-junction of paths, turn right towards some mature beechwood. Just inside this, turn left onto a winding path which climbs for $\frac{1}{3}$ mile, until you reach a stile into a cottage garden.

15

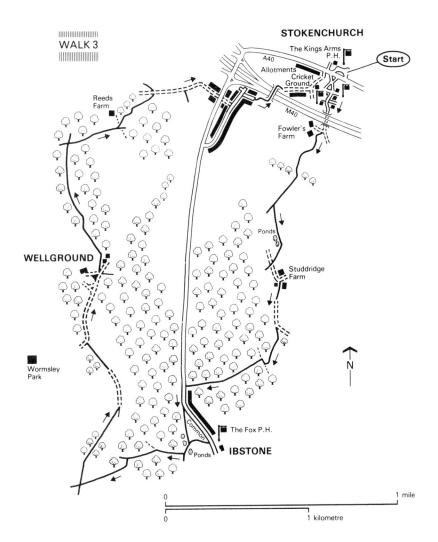

STOKENCHURCH

The Kings Arms P.H.

Start

A40

Allotments

Cricket Ground

M40

Reeds Farm

Fowler's Farm

Ponds

WELLGROUND

Studdridge Farm

N

Wormsley Park

Common

The Fox P.H.

Ponds

IBSTONE

0   1 mile

0   1 kilometre

Cross the garden to the front gate and turn left onto the road into Ibstone.

At a left-hand bend, fork half right off the road and follow an ill-defined bridleway across the back of Ibstone Common, passing two ponds to the right. When you reach the junction with an obvious bridleway leading into woods, turn right. Just inside the wood, take the centre track of a three-way fork. Ignoring crossing tracks and lesser branching tracks, follow the track which after about 200 yards enters a deep descending gulley. Some 200 yards down this gulley,

16

turn left onto a waymarked path, crossing the bank, then dropping steeply to a stile leading out into a field.

Here a view opens out over the tranquil southern end of the Wormsley Valley with Northend on a distant ridge. Turn right and follow a fence and sporadic hedge downhill to a crossing hedge. Here a right turn through a double gate brings you onto a bridleway which forms the spine of the rights of way network in the valley. Follow the left-hand hedge, ignoring the first gate in it. On reaching a second gate, go through it and continue between hedges and trees until re-emerging into the open. A few yards further on, follow a track along the left-hand side of a hedge. Where this ends, continue straight on with a copse to the left and the remains of a fence to the right until you reach a bend in a rough road. Continue straight on along this road, glancing through the trees to the left, for a view of Wormsley Park House. After just over half a mile, a cottage on the left marks your arrival at the tiny hamlet of Wellground.

At a junction of several tracks and paths just beyond the cottage, fork half left onto a footpath passing a garage. Follow the path which climbs gently into woodland for just over $\frac{1}{2}$ mile, until a waymarked crossing path is reached. Turn right and follow this over a rise, then descend out of the wood. Follow the edge of the wood for a short distance and continue straight on across the field to a former gateway into another wood. Here fork half left and, ignoring a crossing track to Reeds Farm, follow a winding waymarked path uphill until you emerge onto a rough road at the far corner of the wood. Join the road and follow it for $\frac{1}{4}$ mile, crossing a field and continuing along a lane, until you reach a road. Cross the road and continue straight on along a path to another road. Turn left onto this and just before its end, turn right into Green Lane. Continue, crossing the M40 by a footbridge, for nearly $\frac{1}{2}$ mile, until you reach the A40 near the starting point.

Walk 4   Saunderton Station

5¼ miles (8.5 km)

Start: Saunderton station approach; O S map ref. 813981
Heavy nettle growth may be encountered in the summer months.

Saunderton station would seem to be most curiously situated, being
more than 2½ miles from the principal hamlets of this scattered parish
which are, in fact, considerably closer to Princes Risborough station!
Rather than the station being built to serve Saunderton village, a new
settlement with several factories has grown up around the station.
The walk, which in contrast to many in the Chilterns is very open in
nature, takes you along the wide Saunderton Valley to Saunderton
Lee near Lodge Hill, before climbing over Bledlow Ridge to Radnage
Church in its secluded valley. It returns over another part of Bledlow
Ridge to Slough Hill and Saunderton station.
   Saunderton station, 4½ miles northwest of High Wycombe, may be
reached from the town by taking the A40 westwards for two miles,
then forking right onto the A4010 and following it for 2½ miles. Turn
left onto a road signposted to Saunderton Bottom and Deanfield and
after passing under a railway bridge, turn immediately right into the
station approach. There is space for parking at weekends, when no
trains stop at Saunderton, but on weekdays it may be necessary to
find a space elsewhere.
   Starting from Saunderton station approach, go down the approach
and turn right into Slough Lane. On reaching a left-hand hairpin
bend near some cottages, turn right into a field entrance, then bear
immediately left through a hedge gap and follow the right-hand hedge
straight on towards the corner of the field. Just before reaching it, turn
right through a gap in the hedge and cross the corner of the next field,
rejoining the hedge at the top of a rise. Follow the hedge straight on for
a few yards. Where it turns right, go straight on across the field,
rejoining the hedge by the corner of Molins' factory fence. Here continue along a wide track between the hedge and the fence to Haw
Lane. Cross this and go straight on through a hedge gap and across a
field, walking parallel to the railway to your right until, level with
Grange Farm on the other side of the railway, you reach a grassy track
from the farm. Here bear slightly left across the field, heading towards
two distant electricity pylons, to a stile under a blackthorn tree. Cross
the stile and follow the right-hand hedge to Manor Farm, Saunderton
Lee. Here bear half right onto a track through the hedge, ignoring a
right-hand turn into the farmyard, and continue straight on past a
thatched cottage and through two gates.

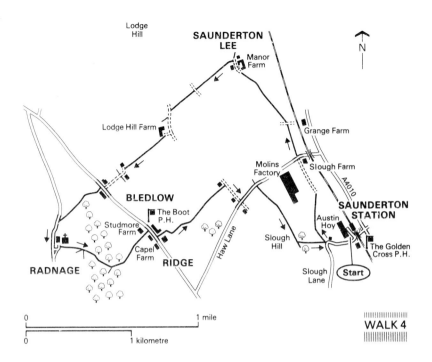

After the second gate at the corner of the farm, turn left and follow the left-hand fence and hedge until you reach a stile at the base of a pylon. Cross the stile and continue straight on, following a right-hand hedge, to a crossing grassy track by a hedge. Lodge Hill, to the right, has a rather unusual appearance, rising up on its own out of the Saunderton Valley and not being part of a Chiltern ridge. It is of interest for a number of ancient earthworks and the discovery there of Neolithic tools, Bronze Age pottery and other relics.

Continue straight on over a stile and across the next field on the line of a crop break to a bridleway beside the next hedge. Turn left onto this and follow it past Lodge Hill Farm to the right. Then turn right onto a macadam farm road leading to a barn at the far end of the farm. By the barn, turn left through double gates, then bear half right across a field to a stile, where two hedges and a fence meet. Cross the stile and heading slightly right of diagonally go uphill across a field, making for a stile under some trees left of a house, when these come into view. Here cross the stile and go straight on up a lane to the spine road of Bledlow Ridge.

Turn right onto the road, and where the houses to the left end, turn left over a stile and follow the left-hand hedge downhill. In the corner of the field, cross a stile into a thicket and continue straight on through

19

this, soon emerging in a scrubby downland field. Follow the right-hand hedge downhill to a stile in bushes in the bottom corner. Cross this stile and continue straight on across the next field to a stile into a road. Turn left onto the road and after 300 yards turn left again up the drive to Radnage Church.

Go straight on through a gate into the churchyard. The thirteenth-century church has a Saxon font dug up in a field nearby and is notable for a thirteenth-century mural, discovered beneath later murals during restoration work.

Bear right of the church to a stile in the stone wall at the back corner of the churchyard. Having crossed this, bear half right across a field to another stile. Bear slightly left across the next field to where the bottom edge of a wood appears to drop down. On reaching this, go through what actually is a narrow gap between woods into a scrubby downland field. Follow the left-hand edge of this field uphill through bushes with magnificent views behind towards Radnage City, Stokenchurch, Andridge and the back of the escarpment, and enter the wood at the top corner of the field. Go straight on through the wood, crossing a stile, and on reaching the corner of a field, ignore a branching path to the right and bear left into a path between a hedge and a fence and follow this path to Bledlow Ridge.

Here turn right along the road. Opposite Capel Farm, turn left into another path between a fence and a hedge and follow this to a stile. Cross this and follow the left-hand hedge downhill. Where the hedge turns left, bear half right across the field to a stile in the corner. Having crossed this, follow the right-hand hedge downhill to a stile by which you may cross the hedge. Then follow the other side of the hedge downhill to a corner. Here continue straight on across the field to a stile and gate to the right of a bungalow. Having crossed the stile, turn right into a rough lane and follow it to a road. Turn left here. At the top of a rise, turn right through a hedge gap and follow the right-hand hedge uphill. At the top of Slough Hill go through a hedge gap and, after the first left-hand tree, turn left through the hedge and bear half right across a field to a hedge gap in front of a cottage, from which you retrace your steps to Saunderton station.

Walk 5   Piddington (Bucks)

5¾ miles (9.5 km)

Start: Dashwood Arms, Piddington; O S map ref. 808943

Piddington, just off the Oxford (A40) road, is an unusual Chiltern village in a number of ways. Dominated by a tall factory chimney and built largely of red brick on a hillside rather than in a valley bottom or on a hilltop, it would seem more typical of West Yorkshire than the Chilterns. This is because, like many West Yorkshire villages, it is a late product of the industrial revolution. North's furniture factory was built here in 1903, when his previous premises in West Wycombe became too small and Sir George Dashwood, who owned the village, objected to the erection of a larger factory there with such a chimney. A number of houses, which form the nucleus of the present village, were built at the same time to house the factory workers. Old locals tell how many more used to walk up to five miles from surrounding villages to put in a 10½-hour day at the factory. The walk follows the footsteps of many of these workers, soon leaving this rural industrial outpost behind and traversing little-used paths through quiet Chiltern backland with some superb views across the hilltops and a wealth of pleasant woodland.

Piddington, 3½ miles west of High Wycombe, may be reached from the town by following the A40 towards Oxford and turning left to the village on a loop road which marks the former course of the road, before the village was bypassed. Cars can be parked at various points along this loop road, but the car park behind the Dashwood Arms should not be used, as it is a private car park for customers and users of the recreation ground only.

Starting from the Dashwood Arms at the western end of the Piddington loop road turn left into the Wheeler End road. In a few yards, just past a cottage, turn right onto a rough track through a gate. Follow the winding track beside a left-hand hedge to Fillington Farm, where it twists somewhat to the right, but does not enter the farm, and goes through a gate. Continue straight on, following a left-hand hedge through another gate. Where the hedge then turns right, turn left through the second of two adjacent gates and follow a left-hand fence to a stile into a belt of trees. Cross this stile, fork immediately left in the tree belt and follow a left-hand hedge uphill. After a short distance, the hedge and path gradually enter a combe, passing a thick hedge climbing the hill to the left. About 60 yards beyond this, turn left over an inconspicuous stile in the hedge. Bear half right up a bank to a gate in the top right-hand corner of the field. Go through this and follow a track across a field over the top of the hill.

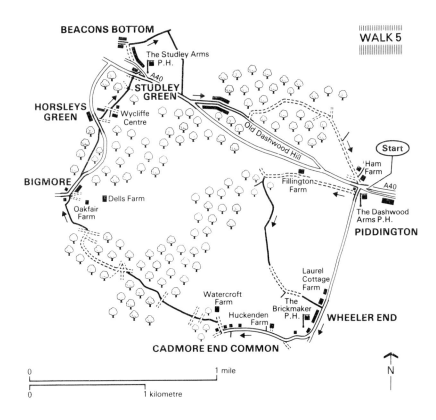

BEACONS BOTTOM

The Studley Arms
P.H.

A40

STUDLEY GREEN

HORSLEYS GREEN

Wycliffe Centre

Old Dashwood Hill

Start

Ham Farm

A40

Fillington Farm

BIGMORE

Dells Farm

Oakfair Farm

The Dashwood Arms P.H.

PIDDINGTON

Laurel Cottage Farm

Watercroft Farm

The Brickmaker P.H.

Huckenden Farm

WHEELER END

CADMORE END COMMON

0   1 mile

0   1 kilometre

N

At the hilltop, before continuing it is well worthwhile standing still and surveying the panoramic views. Follow the track where it joins a fence, bearing slightly left to a stile and gate. Cross the stile and head for the right-hand end of the farm buildings at Laurel Cottage Farm ahead. Keeping right of the farm, follow the path, crossing several stiles by the buildings. The path curves to the left to emerge at a road at Wheeler End by its extensive common.

Turn right along the road, passing the Brickmaker and some attractive cottages. At the end of the cottages, turn right onto another road and follow it for $\frac{1}{2}$ mile to the end of the macadam section by the drive to Watercroft Farm. Turn right into this macadam drive. Then, by a telegraph pole, turn left over a stile and head for the right-hand corner of a wood. Follow the edge of the wood straight on to a stile into the wood. Cross this stile and follow a well-defined path to two stiles at a track. Cross these and continue through a finger of woodland until you leave it by a further stile. Go straight on downhill to a gap in

22

a hedge leading into Leygroves Wood. Follow a winding waymarked path through the wood, which soon crosses a track and climbs slowly to a stile leading into a plantation. At the far side of the plantation, join a fire break and follow this straight on, ignoring all branching tracks. The fire break soon narrows into a track which eventually leaves the wood by a gate. Having left the wood, go straight on through a second gate, then turn left and follow a left-hand fence, and later a hedge, round two sides of a field. You emerge by a house onto a bend in a road at Bigmore.

Ignoring two farm tracks to the right, turn right along the road. Just inside a wood, fork left onto an obvious waymarked path, descending, climbing again and rejoining the road. At the top of the hill, where the road leaves the wood at Horsleys Green, turn right into a track, then immediately left over a stile. Follow the right-hand hedge, crossing two more stiles, to a drive at the Wycliffe Centre. Turn right onto this. Turn left by a tree and a postbox onto a path between a fence and a hedge and follow this into a wood. In the wood, disregard branching paths to left and right and continue straight on out to the A40 at Studley Green. Cross this, bearing slightly right, then turn sharp left by the Studley Arms into a lane. Having passed Mary Towerton School, turn right into another lane and follow it downhill into Beacon's (formerly Bacon's) Bottom.

At the bottom of the hill, turn right through a gate into a field. Follow the left-hand fence along the valley bottom on what is believed to be the oldest route of the Wycombe–Stokenchurch road to a gate into scrubby woodland. Go through this gate. Turn right onto a path which soon leaves the wood by a stile. Climbing steeply, follow the right-hand hedge to another stile at the top. Continue straight on, following the right-hand hedge and crossing a series of stiles, until you reach the A40. Turn left onto this and almost immediately left again onto a road called Old Dashwood Hill which was replaced by the present less steep A40 in the 1920s. Follow this for over $\frac{1}{4}$ mile and, just after woodland begins to the right, turn left onto a track into the wood. After passing a narrow strip of plantation to the right, bear right into a gradually deepening gulley track in mature woodland and follow this downhill. This is believed to be the route of a road which replaced the Beacons Bottom route; it was later replaced in turn by the Old Dashwood Hill route, when the turnpike road to Oxford was constructed in 1744. Eventually the gulley becomes less deep and levels out on leaving the wood. Continue straight on, following a left-hand hedge, rejoining the original route of the road at a hedge gap. At Ham Farm, go through double gates straight on out to the A40 at Piddington.

Walk 6   Lane End

5 miles (8 km)

Start: Lane End public car park; O S map ref. 807918

Lane End, like many Chiltern 'ends', is built around common land at an ancient parish boundary. In Lane End's case however no less than five old parishes, one of which used to be in Oxfordshire, were involved and being at the crossroads of two locally important roads, it is no wonder that its early development was somewhat haphazard and more rapid than in the case of other 'ends'. This is probably the reason for the profusion of scattered Victorian red brick cottages which have made the place so inviting to modern planners for in-filling. Whatever faults one may find with the way the village has developed, two positive features are worth noting: the amount of well-maintained common in and around the village and the attractive thirteenth-century style church built on the site of an earlier building in 1878.

The walk takes in some remote countryside south-east of the village, including picturesque Bluey's Farm in its deep valley, several viewpoints, much woodland walking and the site of an ancient chapel which may have been the nucleus of a lost village.

Lane End, $3\frac{1}{2}$ miles southwest of High Wycombe, may be reached by leaving the M40 at Junction 4 (Handy Cross, Wycombe Central) and turning north towards Cressex Industrial Estate from which a route is signposted. Free parking is available in the rear part of the public car park on the north side of the B482 just west of the central crossroads.

Starting from Lane End public car park, cross the B482 and take a gravel track opposite by the village hall. On emerging onto the common near the church, head for the right-hand end of the churchyard wall. Follow a path alongside the wall past the church. At the end of the churchyard, go straight on, joining a track and passing the Jolly Blacksmith. Continue to follow the track round the back of the common until you join a road by a garage. Turn right along the road and follow it for some 200 yards, until a common opens out to the left. Turn left here onto a macadam drive to Moor Farm which is in part seventeenth-century. Just before the farm, fork left to a stile under an ash tree. Cross this stile and go straight on across a field to another stile in a hedge, some way right of a gate. Having crossed this, bear slightly left past a telegraph pole to a stile at the corner of a wood. Inside the wood, follow its edge for about 150 yards. Where the edge of the wood turns away, go straight ahead on what becomes a sunken track, then leave the wood by a stile into a field on the other side.

24

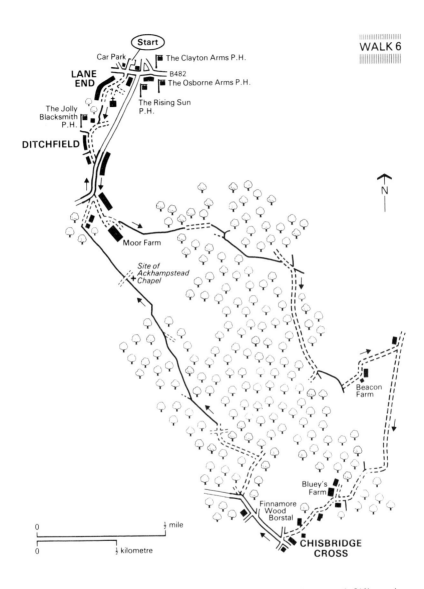

Bear slightly right here, following the edge of the wood. Where it turns left, bear half right into the wood to pick up an obvious path, onto which you turn left. After about ¼ mile, the path joins a track and bears slightly right. Where the track and the valley bottom which it follows turn right, ignore branches to the left and continue to follow the track. For a while it joins the edge of the wood, and then re-enters it. Shortly after emerging onto the edge of the wood for a second time, where the track turns right, turn left across a stile. Bear half right up a very steep bank to the end of a hedge on the skyline. From the top of this bank there is a view of Bluey's Farm in its peaceful wooded valley, making the steep climb worthwhile.

Bear half left into a fenced cattle drive and follow this to a gate at Beacon Farm. Turn left here onto a farm track which swings right around the farm buildings and follows a hedge to a gate by a cottage. Go through this gate and turn right onto a hedged bridleway. Follow this for $\frac{2}{3}$ mile. After entering a wood and going downhill, you reach Bluey's Farm. Continue straight on through the farm. Follow a macadam farm road uphill, ignoring branches to the right which lead to farm buildings and Finnamore Wood Borstal. You eventually reach a crossroads at the tiny hamlet of Chisbridge Cross with a thatched cottage opposite.

Turn right onto the main road here and follow it for $\frac{1}{4}$ mile, ignoring a right turn into the borstal and a left turn by a cottage. Then, at a left-hand bend, turn right onto a track into the woods and take the right fork. Follow this track for some 300 yards until it forks again. Here turn left onto a wide track through a plantation. Where this track enters a mature wood, ignore a crossing track and go straight on, entering another plantation. At the far side of this, fork right. Continue straight on for $\frac{1}{4}$ mile, until joining a track at a stile and gate at the edge of the wood. Cross the stile and bear slightly right across the field to a set of wooden rails in a gap in the hedge on the skyline. Having crossed these, turn left along the hedge and follow it to a corner of the field by a clump of trees, where the path continues straight on between hedges to a stile.

The hedged area to the right containing the clump of trees is the site of Ackhampstead Chapel, an ancient chapel built before 1241 and demolished in 1849. The chapel served as a chapel-of-ease for the manor of Ackhampstead, until 1895 a detached manor of Lewknor parish, Oxfordshire. It can be assumed to have formerly had more houses than modern Moor End, otherwise the building of the chapel would not have been necessary. The location of these houses is however uncertain.

Cross the stile, a rough lane and another stile and go straight on across a field to a stile well left of the cottages ahead. On crossing this, follow a path hugging a garden wall until you emerge from the scrub onto a lane. Go straight on along the lane to a road at the start of the drive to Moor Farm. From here retrace your outward route to Lane End.

Walk 7   Cadmore End

5¾ miles (9 km)

Start: Cadmore End church; O S map ref. 784925

Cadmore End, like many Chiltern 'ends', is built around an ancient common at an equally ancient parish boundary. Like many such settlements, Cadmore End is distinctly higgledy-piggledy with stretches of common separating its scattered clusters of cottages. The church, although built in 1851, is of a thirteenth-century design in traditional Chiltern flint.

The village, situated five miles west of High Wycombe, may be reached by leaving the M40 at Junction 5 (Stokenchurch), following the A40 into Stokenchurch, forking right onto the B482 towards Marlow and following this for 2½ miles. By Cadmore End School, ⅓ mile beyond the Blue Flag, turn right into a cul-de-sac to Cadmore End church. Cars can be parked at various points along this road.

Starting from the end of the macadam road by Cadmore End church, follow its stony continuation, bearing left and passing clusters of cottages, for ¼ mile until you emerge onto the B482 opposite the Old Ship. Turn right along this. At the top of the hill, opposite a lane and a double cottage, turn right onto the track to Rackley's Farm. Fork almost immediately right through the garden gate of a bungalow and cross the garden diagonally to a stile. Having crossed this, go straight on across a small field to a pond in the corner. Cross a stile into a path between a hedge and a fence and follow this to another stile which leads into a field. Continue straight on beside a hedge until wooden rails lead into a copse on the right. Follow a winding path taking you on to another stile. Cross this and turn right across the corner of a field to a double stile. Having crossed this, go straight on across the next field making for a telegraph pole in the hedge ahead, roughly halfway between the bend in a road and a distant flint cottage. Here bear right along the hedge. Cross a stile in the corner of the field, then continue straight on beside a hedge to another stile leading into a lane. Go straight on along the lane, ignoring a left-hand branch to a farm in the valley. Join a bridleway coming out of a wood to the right and follow it to a stile ahead at a sharp left-hand bend.

From this stile the picturesque village of Fingest comes into view ahead clustered in a hollow where four valleys meet. The significance of the village's location is reflected in its name, originally 'Tinghurst', meaning 'meeting place in a spinney'. Its church is of particular interest as it is a largely unaltered twelfth-century structure, unusually narrow, with thick plastered walls and a tower with a twin-

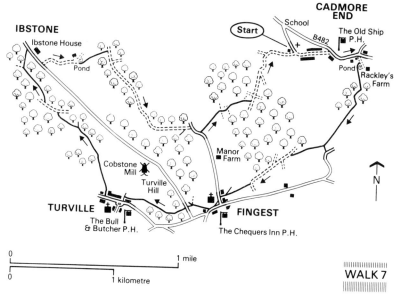

gabled roof. Behind the trees on a hilltop to the right can be seen Cobstone Windmill, which has featured in various films.

Cross the stile and continue straight on beside a fence to a double stile. Having crossed this, follow a hedge to another stile by which you enter an alleyway to a village street. Turn left onto the road, then fork right through a kissing-gate. Passing the seventeenth-century Chequers Inn to the left, cross the churchyard diagonally to another kissing-gate into a road. A few yards along the road fork right into a path between a wall and a fence. Follow this, climbing gently, into a wood. Here fork left, soon crossing a road and stile, and take a confined path for $\frac{1}{4}$ mile with Turville Hill to the right and a narrow belt of trees to the left concealing the Hambleden Valley. At the end of this section, cross a stile and a few yards ahead, Turville comes into view in the valley.

Turville is another picturesque village. The name belies its French sound, being a corruption of the Anglo-Saxon 'Thyrefeld' meaning 'Thyri's field'. The church, whose fabric is in part eleventh-century, has been much rebuilt and renovated over the centuries and is associated with a gruesome mystery. During renovation work in 1900, an old stone coffin was found hidden beneath the floor containing not only the skeleton of a thirteenth-century priest, but also the later remains of a woman with a bullet-hole in her skull!

Bear half left across the field to a stile by an iron gate. Cross this and follow the right-hand fence to another stile. Then turn left along a track to the village green, the epitome of Chiltern tradition, surrounded by church, pub and a number of brick, flint and timber cottages. Turn right along the village street. Opposite a black barn with a small turret on the roof, turn right between the cottages onto the path to Barn Cottage. Passing the cottage, climb steps and cross a stile. Bear half left across the field to a stile in the far corner. Cross the stile and the corner of another field to a stile which leads into a belt of trees. Once among the trees, bear right to a further stile, then bear half left, following a winding path across a field and over two more stiles into a wood. Follow the fence, along the edge of the wood, to its end. Here enter the wood and join a track bearing left. Just past the end of the left-hand plantation, turn right onto a waymarked path. After some 200 yards, ignore a stile to the right entering a plantation, but turn right when the rough track on which you now are swings away to the left.

At the far side of the plantation, turn right onto a road, passing eighteenth-century Ibstone House, former home of the authoress, Dame Rebecca West. At the end of its garden, turn left through iron gates into a lane. At the end of the lane by a barn, bear right through a wooden gate, then left along a fence downhill to a gate into a belt of trees. Once among the trees, turn right onto a track and follow it along the valley bottom, ignoring all branching tracks for $\frac{3}{4}$ mile, until you reach a road at Gravesend. Turn right onto the road. At a right-hand bend, turn left over a stile and go straight across a field climbing to a stile which leads into a wood. Inside the wood, a fire-break is being created at the time of writing which will lead you uphill. By an oak tree in its midst, fork right. Now continue straight on until you reach a crossing track. Here turn left and continue straight on. At the gate at the edge of the wood, the track merges with another track; follow this winding track uphill back to Cadmore End.

Walk 8   Southend

5 miles (8 km)

Start: The Drover, Southend; O S map ref. 752898

Southend, a scattered hamlet on a plateau on the Bucks–Oxon county boundary with magnificent views to the northeast across the Turville valley towards Fingest, Turville, Cobstone Mill and Cadmore End, derives its name from its geographical position at the southern end of Turville parish. Like many other such hilltop outposts of southern Chiltern parishes, Southend is built around a common, where hilltop clay was quarried for brickmaking. The walk itself includes one of the finest Chiltern paths through Stonor Park giving clear views of historic Stonor House and the escarpment backland, as well as crossing the plateau at Bosmore Farm with its panoramic views to the south across the Thames Valley to Berkshire and beyond.

Southend, 4½ miles north of Henley, may be reached by leaving the M40 at Junction 5 (Stokenchurch) and taking the road signposted to Ibstone, following this for four miles to its end at Fingest. Here turn right towards Turville and take the second turning left signposted to Turville Heath. At Turville Heath turn left onto a road signposted to Southend and on reaching it, turn left by the Drover pub. Ample verges are available here for parking.

Starting from the Drover, head south along the road and on passing a cottage on the right, turn right onto a track between the cottage and a wood. A few yards along this track on the right-hand side is a large metal drum, a charcoal burner which was used until about ten years ago for a traditional Chiltern industry. On leaving the field to the right behind, the track enters a plantation. Ignoring branching tracks, follow it straight on for some 300 yards. By a large pine, fork left off the track onto a narrow path through the plantation. At the far side of the plantation, go through a giant kissing-gate in a high wire-mesh deer fence into Stonor Park and follow an obvious waymarked path through an area of mature trees and scrubland, until this finally emerges into open parkland.

In the Middle Ages, Stonor Park was renowned for the quality of its venison and even today it is noted for its large herd of fallow deer. Stonor House, despite the relatively modern appearance of its red brick eighteenth-century facade, is of considerable antiquity. Much of the house and chapel was built in 1280, but over the centuries considerable renovations have occurred particularly to the exterior. Throughout this time, the house has been the property of the Stonors, a noted Catholic family, which successfully laid claim to the Camoys

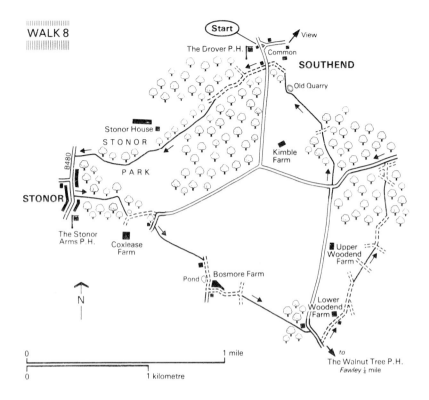

barony in 1838. During the Reformation, a number of secret passages were constructed to hide Catholic fugitives, amongst whom was Edmund Campion.

Having crossed a wide clearing created to improve the view from the front of the house, the obvious path winds through some trees and drops down to a kissing-gate in a corner of the park. On reaching the B480 road here, turn left onto it and follow it past the Maidensgrove turning into Stonor village.

Prior to 1896, the village was a detached manor of distant Pyrton parish, and was known as Upper Assendon. Although some new development has taken place, Stonor has managed to maintain the character set by its sixteenth- to eighteenth-century cottages.

Just past some pine trees, turn left onto a bridleway between garden fences. This soon joins the Stonor Park deer fence and follows it steeply uphill through woodland. On reaching a fork at the top of the hill by a pond just inside the park, go left and continue to follow the deer fence. There are good views to the right across the Thames Valley towards the distant Hampshire Downs. You reach a right-angle bend in a narrow road; turn right, and opposite a cottage gate,

31

turn left over a stile and bear half right across the field to another stile. From here, make for the left-hand of two telegraph poles left of a cottage on the skyline, where a stile leads onto a macadam farm road. Turn right onto this passing the cottage and a pond to the right and Bosmore Farm to the left. At some white gates, turn left onto a track passing between farm buildings and then swinging right out of the farm. Follow the track until it turns sharp right. Here cross a stile and follow a power-line to another stile in the valley bottom. Cross this and continue uphill through scrubby woodland until you reach a meadow. The path crosses this and follows the garden fence and hedge to the right of a house out to a road.

Turn right onto the road. After 100 yards, turn left onto the drive to Lower Woodend Farm and, ignoring forks to the left, follow it to a gate. Go through the gate, and just past a shed turn right onto a track which soon swings left across the field to another gate. Here the track joins another. Where it later bends to the left, bear slightly right, leaving the track, and head for the right-hand end of a line of six oaks to the right of a tree covered in ivy in the next hedge. Cross a bridleway here and continue straight on to a gap where two hedges meet. Go through the gap and follow a track along a hedge to the corner of a wood. Bearing slightly right, follow the track along the edge of the wood. Enter the wood by a gate and follow a waymarked path straight on to a road. Here turn left along the road.

At a road junction, turn right over a stile and go straight across a field to a stile into a wood. Inside the wood bear slightly left and follow an obvious path downhill to a bridlegate onto a bridleway. Cross this bridleway and continue uphill inside the edge of a wood to a stile into a field. Bear slightly left along what is normally a crop break and follow this until you reach an old quarry surrounded by trees. Go round the left side of this, then cross the field to a stile and gate into a lane. Follow the lane until you reach a road. Turn right here for the Drover.

Walk 18 Checkendon Church

Walk 3
Pond on Ibstone
Common

Walk 14
The Almshouses,
Ewelme

Walk 27
River Wye at
Wooburn Green

Walk 9   Watlington Hill

2½ or 5¼ miles (4 or 8.5 km)

Start: Watlington Hill car park; O S map ref. 710936

Watlington Hill, one of the finest viewpoints on the Chiltern escarpment, is one of many open space properties owned by the National Trust. This has benefited the walker by ensuring public access, and Trust volunteers have created paths across it, cleared scrub, excluded horses which formerly damaged its turf and taken other conservation measures.

The ancient market town of Watlington, dating back to at least the sixth century, has a fourteenth-century church which was extensively 'restored' in the 1870s, a seventeenth-century town hall and a wealth of other sixteenth- to eighteenth-century buildings. It is well worth exploring before or after the walk.

Both walks start by crossing the hill and reascend the escarpment by the combe to the north of it, while the longer walk takes in some remote woodland.

Watlington Hill, 1¼ miles east of the town (itself six miles north-east of Wallingford), may be reached by leaving the M40 at Junction 6 (Lewknor) and following the B4009 south-west for 2¾ miles to Watlington town centre. A left turn signposted to Christmas Common leads you up Watlington Hill to a signposted car park at the top of the hill.

Take the path signposted from the car park to the hilltop. Follow this down a few steps (cut by Chiltern Society volunteers) and then along the roadside verge for a few yards, until a stile leads you through scrub out onto the open hillside. From here, follow an ill-defined path along the ridge just below the patches of scrub on the ridge top, until the path becomes more obvious through some gorse bushes. On reaching the gorse bushes the path, which now follows the most obvious course, begins to descend at first gradually and then more steeply. After some 300 yards of the steepest section, you pass a folly known as the White Mark. This is a representation of an obelisk, 270 feet long and 36 feet wide, cut into the chalk slope on the orders of Edward Horne of Greenfield in 1764. Just below the White Mark the path crosses a clearing to a stile. Having crossed this, turn left between some conifers and thick scrub and continue until you join a road at a bend at the foot of the hill.

Opposite the first bungalow on the left-hand side, turn right onto the Upper Icknield Way. This is an ancient Celtic road, now a grassy track, which has in recent times found a new role as part of the modern long distance Ridgeway Path. Follow this for ½ mile. Turn

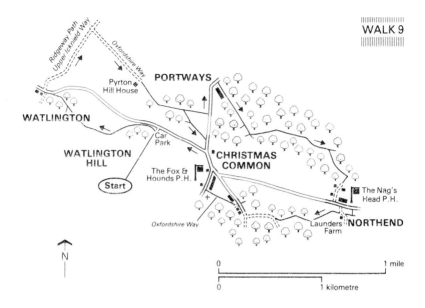

PORTWAYS

Pyrton
Hill House

WATLINGTON

Car
Park

WATLINGTON
HILL

The Fox &
Hounds P.H.

CHRISTMAS
COMMON

Start

The Nag's
Head P.H.

Oxfordshire Way

Launders
Farm

NORTHEND

N

0   1 mile

0   1 kilometre

right onto a rough macadam and gravel crossing track traditionally known as the Pyrton Driftway because of its former use for driving sheep from Pyrton village to downland pasture on Pyrton Hill. It is now part of the CPRE's long distance path, the Oxfordshire Way. After nearly $\frac{1}{2}$ mile the macadam surface ends at Pyrton Hill House. Here continue straight on along an unsurfaced bridleway climbing steadily, until you enter a belt of thick scrub.

Where the path forks some way inside the scrub, walkers wishing to do the shorter walk should go right, following the Oxfordshire Way. On leaving the scrub, cross a stile and bear half right to another stile under the larger trees in a hedge. Do not cross the stile, but follow the hedge crossing two other stiles until reaching a road. Turn right onto the road and turn almost immediately right again onto a road sign-posted to Watlington which leads back to the car park.

At the fork in the path walkers wishing to do the longer walk should continue straight on along the bridleway until reaching a road. Here turn left onto the road and follow it passing a farm and cottages in a field on the right known as Portways. On rounding a sharp right-hand bend, turn right onto a waymarked footpath into the woods behind Portways. Follow this along the fence of a plantation and then in a generally straight direction through mature beechwoods until reaching a small pit. Here the path swings left and right around the pit. Soon afterwards, where you come to a field on the right, fork left onto another waymarked path going downhill and deeper into the wood. After $\frac{1}{4}$ mile the path emerges into clear-felled woodland known as Blackmoor Wood through which it continues for a further $\frac{1}{4}$ mile. Just after the beginning of a field to the left, a path branches to the right. Follow this path steeply uphill until reaching a stile out of the wood by a pit. Cross this, then cross a narrow field and another stile into a lane. Follow the lane out to a road at Northend.

Turn left onto the road passing the Nag's Head and then turn right onto a bridleway across Northend Common. At a T-junction turn right again. On emerging from the common, go straight on past Launder's Farm. Where the track turns right, leave it and continue straight on through a gate and along a hedgerow until you reach a gate into a wood. Go through this, then fork right and follow a way-marked path straight on through a plantation and under a wooden rail into a mature beechwood. Continue straight on downhill. At the bottom of the hill join a track, ignoring a branch to the left, and follow this uphill until you reach a rough Saxon lane, known as Hollandridge Lane, at the top of the hill. Turn right onto this lane which soon becomes macadamed and follow it until you reach a stile in the right-hand fence. Here turn left onto a track between cottage gardens. Having passed these, fork right onto a path through a plantation which comes out on a road by Christmas Common church, a chapel-of-ease built in 1891. The name Christmas Common is believed to be derived from the signing of a Christmas truce here in the Civil War in 1643. Turn right onto the road passing the Fox & Hounds and follow this for $\frac{1}{4}$ mile. Then turn left onto a road sign-posted to Watlington which leads back to the car park.

Walk 10   Russell's Water

8 miles (12.5 km)

Start: Russell's Water village pond; O S map ref. 708898
In summer part of the route may be overgrown with nettles

Russell's Water, situated on a ridge-top plateau about $1\frac{1}{2}$ miles from
the Chiltern escarpment, is named after a local brickmaker and his
pond in the centre of the village. It is believed to be a relatively modern
settlement which grew up around the common (for which it is best
known today) as a result of the pressures of land enclosure.

This walk combines spectacular escarpment downland with
remote Chiltern beechwoods and is particularly attractive in the
bluebell season (mid-May).

Russell's Water, $5\frac{1}{2}$ miles north-west of Henley, may be reached
from the A423 by turning north onto the B481 at Nettlebed, following
this for $2\frac{3}{4}$ miles towards Watlington, and then taking a road signposted to Russell's Water on the right. Cars may be parked on the
Common or greens within 15 feet of highways.

Starting from Russell's Water village pond, head southwards along
the road until you reach a small green on the left. By a small disused
chapel opposite this, turn right into a rough lane and follow it past a
white house with shutters, descending slowly at first. At a gate
directly ahead, turn sharp right and follow the lane steeply downhill
to the bottom of the valley. On reaching a T-junction with another
lane, turn right and ignoring turnings and gates to right and left,
follow this lane, Law Lane, through a belt of trees and a copse, then
past a few houses to the B481 road at Cookley Green.

Cookley Green once served as a domicile for farmworkers and
servants at Swyncombe Manor. The next part of the walk follows
their footsteps to work and to church.

Turn left onto the road then almost immediately half right and
follow the row of pines across the back of the village green to a road
junction. Here go straight on along a road until reaching a kissing-
gate on the left about 50 yards after the start of a wood. Fork half left
through this and follow a straight path, ignoring crossing tracks, to
another kissing-gate on the far side of the wood. Go through this to
enter Swyncombe Park with Swyncombe House, an Elizabethan
manor house extensively rebuilt in the last century, becoming visible
through the trees ahead. Follow a depression in the ground straight
on across the park to another kissing-gate under some yew trees. Continue along a waymarked path through the trees and across a drive,
and turn right through a gate into the churchyard of the largely Saxon
St Botolph's Church.

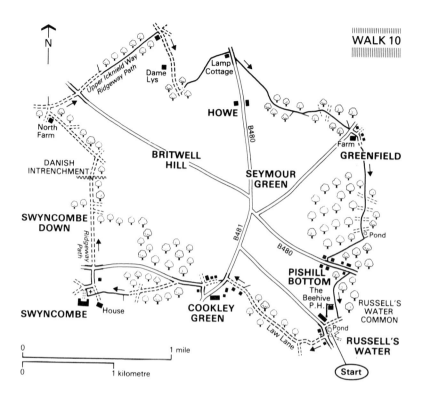

N

Upper Icknield Way
Ridgeway Path

Dame
Lys

Lamp
Cottage

HOWE

B480

North
Farm

DANISH
INTRENCHMENT

BRITWELL
HILL

GREENFIELD

Farm

SEYMOUR
GREEN

SWYNCOMBE
DOWN

Ridgeway
Path

B481

B480

Pond

PISHILL
BOTTOM

The
Beehive
P.H.

SWYNCOMBE

House

COOKLEY
GREEN

RUSSELL'S
WATER
COMMON

Law Lane

Pond

RUSSELL'S
WATER

0   1 mile

0   1 kilometre

Start

At the far side of the churchyard, turn right and follow a lane bearing left to the top of a rise. Cross the road here. Take the Ridgeway Path straight on through a small gate and along a track downhill beside a hedge, then uphill between a wood and a fence until you enter the wood. At the top of the hill, Swyncombe Down, views open out through the trees across the Oxfordshire Plain towards Oxford. The track then descends again to cross a gulley, part of an ancient earthwork known as the Danish Intrenchment. After emerging from the trees and bushes, the path turns left along a belt of trees towards North Farm, with views towards Britwell House on the next rise.

At the far end of the farm buildings turn right through a gap in the trees to the Upper Icknield Way, an ancient Celtic road named after the Iceni, the people of Boadicea. Follow this wide hedged track for nearly a mile, crossing a road. Where the Way has fallen into disuse for wheeled traffic, continue through a belt of scrub until you reach a large new house on the right. Just past this, take the first of two right-hand turnings, a rough macadam drive. Follow this for nearly ½ mile passing Dame Lys Farm (formerly Dame Alice Farm, named after

Alice Chaucer, granddaughter of the poet and Lady of Ewelme Manor in the fifteenth century) where the lane becomes unsurfaced, and a barn and cottage on the left. Having entered a belt of trees, turn left into another lane which soon becomes a narrow winding path between hedges and fences. Follow this until you reach the B480 road by Lamp Cottage.

Turn right onto the road and at the far end of the cottage fence, cross the road and take a path through a gate and alongside a hedge through two fields to a belt of trees. On entering this, a winding path leads you over a rise and into a dip. Ignoring a right-hand branching path, continue uphill again until reaching a fork. Go left here and follow a waymarked path uphill through beechwoods, ignoring crossing tracks, until you reach a gate onto a road at Greenfield.

Cross the road here and continue virtually straight on along a lane left of a green barn and past some cottages until the lane ends at a gate. Through the gate, bear half right through a bridlegate and head for a finger of woodland ahead, where two more bridlegates bring you into the wood. Follow an ill-defined but waymarked path downhill, crossing a track in the bottom and continuing in a more or less straight line over another rise and across another dip. Just past a woodland pond on the left-hand side the path reaches a T-junction with another waymarked, but better-defined path. Turn right here and follow this path for $\frac{1}{4}$ mile gradually going downhill until, after passing through a decrepit gate, you reach a farmyard. From here metal gates lead out onto the B480 road, known here as Patemore Lane, in Pishill Bottom. (Although pronounced 'Pis-hill' with a short 'i', the name is actually a corruption of 'Peas-hill').

Turn left along the road and follow it for about 350 yards past some cottages until you reach a track on the right leading into the woods. Take this track, which soon becomes a path, keeping left where it forks and eventually emerging onto Russell's Water Common. Follow the right-hand edge of the common until you reach a cart track leading off the common. Turn right onto this track and follow it past the Beehive Inn back to Russell's Water pond.

Walk 11   Maidensgrove

$3\frac{1}{2}$ or $5\frac{1}{2}$ miles (6 or 8.5 km)

Start: Russell's Water Common; O S map ref. 718887

Maidensgrove, referred to in several late medieval documents as 'Menygrove', is the collective name for two small hamlets about $\frac{3}{4}$ mile apart, Maidensgrove and Upper Maidensgrove. They are separated by part of the wide expanse of Russell's Water Common. Maidensgrove is the larger with two farms and a number of old cottages as well as several modern properties, while Upper Maidensgrove boasts a farm and a pub. Both the hamlets and the common are situated on a high ridge which affords extensive views over the hilltops and deep valleys. Both walks descend into the upper part of Bix Bottom and the ancient road to Oxford and return from Park Corner at the head of the valley by way of Redpits Manor and Upper Maidensgrove. The longer walk additionally climbs to Nettlebed Common and Nettlebed, returning on a parallel route.

Maidensgrove, $4\frac{1}{2}$ miles north-west of Henley-on-Thames, may be reached from the town by taking the A423 towards Oxford. At the end of the Fair Mile, fork right onto the B480 towards Watlington. At Stonor, turn left into a concealed turn signposted to Maidensgrove and Russell's Water. After one mile, ignore a turning to the left signposted Maidensgrove and continue straight on for $\frac{1}{4}$ mile out onto Russell's Water Common. Park on the verge at a sharp right-hand bend where the road joins the southern hedge of the common and a rough lane leads off the common. Cars may be parked within 15 feet of the road or this lane, but should not obstruct either.

Both walks start from the bend in the road near Maidensgrove on Russell's Water Common and head southwards on a rough lane called Hatch Lane, leaving the common at this point. Where the right-hand hedge ends and the lane bears left, bear half right across a field to a gap just left of a corner of the wood ahead. This woodland in Bix Bottom is part of the Warburg Nature Reserve owned by the Berkshire, Buckinghamshire and Oxfordshire Naturalists Trust and is noted for its rare chalkland plants. Enter the wood, disregarding a branching path to the left, and follow a path straight on along its top edge. Where the edge of the wood drops down to the left, cross a stile and leave the wood. Here bear half left across a field to a stile in a protruding finger of woodland. Cross this and drop steeply through the wood and over another stile. Then bear half right across a field to a gate leading to a junction of lanes, the major one of which is part of the ancient Henley to Oxford road.

Walkers wishing to take the shorter route should go straight on

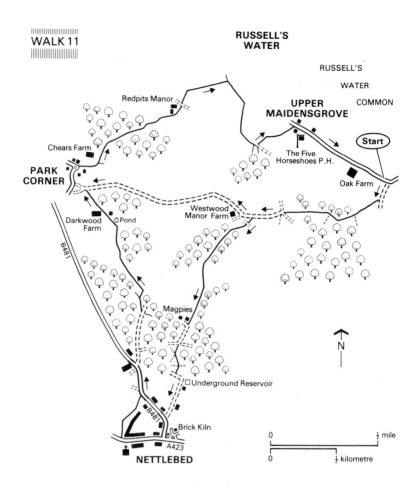

RUSSELL'S

WATER

COMMON

**UPPER
MAIDENSGROVE**

Redpits Manor

Chears Farm

**PARK
CORNER**

The Five
Horseshoes P.H.

Start

Oak Farm

Westwood
Manor Farm

Darkwood
Farm

Pond

B481

Magpies

N

Underground Reservoir

B481

Brick Kiln

A423

NETTLEBED

0   ½ mile

0   ½ kilometre

along the lane and follow it for one mile, soon passing a wood and Westwood Manor Farm to the left and later passing another wood to the left. At a fork just after this, go right. (Now ignore the next two paragraphs).

Walkers wishing to take the longer route should go straight on along the lane, and on reaching the start of a wood to the left, should turn left along the outside of this wood. Cross a track which comes out of the wood, cross a stile and take a path straight on inside the wood. Follow an obvious path through the wood and, on leaving it by a stile, bear half left across a field to the corner of a hedge. Bear half right along the hedge to a stile. Cross this and follow the hedge past a garden and out to a drive at Magpies. Continue straight on along this drive and at a sharp right-hand bend, leave it and go straight on along a path. Where another path crosses diagonally, turn half left onto it and follow it until you reach a major crossing path. Cross this, bearing half right. After passing through gorse bushes, turn left onto a track which leads to the telegraph pole and underground reservoir at the hilltop. Now bear right down a rough lane to the B481 road at Nettlebed.

Turn left onto the B481 and follow it to the A423. Here make a small diversion turning left and left again to reach the old brick kiln. This has been restored in recent years and serves as a monument to the local brick industry which dates back to at least the fifteenth century. Now retrace your steps to the junction of the A423 and B481 and continue straight on along the village high street with its old inns and extensively rebuilt church. At the end of the village, turn right onto a fenced path to the allotments. Keep to the right of these, soon emerging at a bend on the B481. Bear left here and follow the road to a sharp left-hand bend by some council houses. Now fork right onto a stony track through woodland and follow it for $\frac{1}{4}$ mile, ignoring all branching tracks, until you reach a boundary ridge just before the track leaves the wood. Turn half left here onto a defined path and after about 150 yards, having passed under two oak trees, turn right by the second left-hand hazel bush and leave the wood by a stile. Bear left across a field, heading towards Darkwood Farm, to a stile left of a hedge junction in the bottom. Having crossed this, follow a right-hand hedge and later a copse uphill to a white gate. Bear half left here to a stile by a white gate to the left of a cottage, then cross this stile and another. Follow a right-hand fence to a stile by the corner of a wood. Cross this and go straight on along the edge of the wood to a lane. Turn left onto this and then almost immediately fork right.

The long and the short routes are reunited at this point.

Turn right onto a road at Park Corner. and follow it to a sharp left-hand bend. Here turn right onto a hedged bridleway and follow this to a gate and stile. Continue between fences across a field. Then go downhill through a wood and uphill between a hedge and a fence to Redpits Manor. At a crossing track, bear slightly left and enter a hedged bridleway. At the bottom of the hill, turn right onto another similar bridleway. After $\frac{1}{3}$ mile, just before a wood, turn left through a hedge gap and follow a left-hand hedge steeply uphill to a stile. Cross this and continue to follow a left-hand hedge straight on over two more stiles to a road at Upper Maidensgrove. Here turn right and follow the road for $\frac{1}{2}$ mile, passing the Five Horseshoes, back to the point of departure.

Walk 12   Crocker End Green

5¼ miles (8.5 km)

Start: Crocker End Green (east end); O S map ref. 710868

Crocker End, a scattered hamlet separated from Nettlebed by a wooded part of its extensive common, has an attractive village green, around which are to be found most of its picturesque old cottages. Limited modern development has taken place at Catslip nearer the main A423 road. Soundess House, near the village, was the home of Nell Gwynn.

The walk passes through heavily wooded country visiting Bix Bottom with its ruined church, and the hilltop village of Bix; using old trackways which were parts of old routes to Oxford.

Crocker End Green, four miles north-west of Henley-on-Thames, may be reached from the town by following the A423 towards Oxford to a right-hand turn in the woods about a mile west of the Fox at Bix. Turn right here and follow a winding narrow lane for ⅓ mile, until emerging onto the green. Cars can be parked at various points around the green.

Starting from the bend in the road at the eastern end of Crocker End Green, follow a rough track to an old gate at the extreme end of the green. Go through this gate to another gate and stile, with Soundess House coming into view to the left. Cross the stile and follow the right-hand hedge to a stile into an unusual yew wood. Inside the wood, follow an obvious path straight on, disregarding crossing and branching tracks. Eventually you join a forestry track and leave the wood by a redundant stile. Follow the right-hand hedge straight on downhill into Bix Bottom, passing through a gate and later a gate and stile, until reaching a road in the valley bottom.

In the trees to the left are the ruins of a Norman church, built in about 1100 and closed in 1875 on the completion of the church at Bix. This church appears to have been built to serve a village in its immediate vicinity which has since disappeared. This is borne out both by old maps showing a village called Bixbrand on the site and a local farmer finding old bricks in nearby fields and detecting the out-lines of buildings when ploughing. Sited on the original Henley to Oxford road which was superseded by a route over Bix Hill in about 1800, Bixbrand appears to have been deserted in favour of modern Bix on the new road. Bix, however, appears to have been a separate village called Bixgwybynt which also had a medieval church. This church has disappeared without trace and thus the present arrangement would seem to be an amalgamation.

42

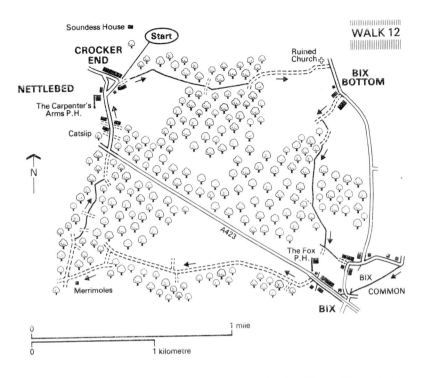

Soundess House
Start
CROCKER
END
Ruined
Church
BIX
BOTTOM
NETTLEBED
The Carpenter's
Arms P.H.
Catslip
A423
The Fox
P.H.
BIX
COMMON
Merrimoles
BIX

0   1 mile
0   1 kilometre

Turn right onto the road and follow it to Valley Farm. Turn right here onto a track between farm buildings. Pass the farmhouse to the right and leave the farm by a gate. Follow a track up a branch of the valley. At a point parallel to the boundary of a wood on the hill to the left, turn left over a stile and follow a fenced path uphill to a stile into the corner of the wood. Inside the wood, turn right onto a track. Where the left-hand edge of the wood bears left away from the track, fork left onto a waymarked path and follow this. Soon you leave the edge of the wood and go more or less straight across it. At the far side of the wood, disregard a stile ahead and bear half left along the inside edge of the wood to a second stile. Cross this and bear slightly left across a field to some gates. Go through one and turn left through the second. Cross two fields, passing through two further gates into a lane at Bix.

Follow this lane out to a bend in a road and continue straight on along the road, soon reaching Bix Common Field. This is one of the rare remaining examples of the once numerous common fields, farmed by various local farmers in rotation. Ignore a turning to the left and follow the road along the edge of the common field to a viewpoint at the far end over the valley towards Henley. Then turn round and follow a footpath diagonally across the common field, heading for a

43

gabled house to the left of the church. At a road junction by the church, take an alleyway left of a telephone box through to the A423. Bear slightly right along its pavement and just before reaching the Fox, cross the road and take a lane opposite known as the Old London Road, part of the initial replacement route for the Bix Bottom road.

Cross a cattle grid and ignore a branching path and macadam drive to the left. After $\frac{2}{3}$ mile in the bottom of a valley, disregard another branching track to the left. At a fork $\frac{1}{3}$ mile further on, go left, leaving the Old London Road. At a right-hand bend, ignore branching tracks to the left. Just past a large house called Merrimoles, turn right at a junction and follow a stony track through woodland until reaching a clearing. Before the clearing an ancient earthwork called Highmoor Trench, which formed part of Grim's Ditch, is crossed. In the clearing turn right onto a grassy track, then at the far side bear slightly left through bushes into the wood and follow a waymarked path straight on. Ignore a crossing track and descend to the Old London Road in the valley bottom. Cross this and follow the waymarked path straight on, climbing again and and soon entering a plantation. At first your path bears left through the plantation, but in the middle of it you turn right and, on leaving the plantation, bear slightly left joining a track and following it out to the A423 road. Cross this and take the road opposite which leads back to Crocker End Green in $\frac{1}{3}$ mile.

Walk 13   Nuffield

$4\frac{1}{2}$ or $8\frac{1}{4}$ miles (7.5 or 13.5 km)

Start: Gangsdown Hill layby, A423; O S map ref. 671880

Nuffield is separated from the A423 by an extensive common, much of
which has been converted into a golf course. The village has a twelfth-
century church and to the north of the main road is Nuffield Place,
former home of William Morris, later Lord Nuffield, who took his title
from the name of the village.

Both the long and the short walk soon leave the main road behind
and lead into some of the remotest countryside in the Chilterns with
fine views of the Berkshire Downs, Vale of the White Horse and
Oxfordshire Plain. This is particularly true of the longer walk which
descends the escarpment to the hamlet of Hailey, where a collection of
antique agricultural implements surrounds the local pub.

Gangsdown Hill layby is situated on the A423 between Henley and
Wallingford about four miles east of Wallingford, halfway up a hill on
the north side of a three-lane section of road. There is ample space for
parking.

Starting from Gangsdown Hill layby, follow the wide verge on the
north side of the road up to the top of the hill. Just past the Crown,
cross the road to a stony track and by an outbuilding of the inn, bear
half left across the golf course. Take care not to cross the fairways
when golfers are driving. Head for a gap in some trees, leading to
another road. Cross this and go straight on to a gap in the next belt of
trees. Then bear slightly right to another gap and go straight on to a
third. By the thirteenth tee, bear half right to a stile in the left-hand
hedge near the corner of a wood. Leaving the golf course behind, cross
this stile and follow the left-hand hedge across a field. At the end of the
field, go through a hedge gap by a telegraph pole and turn right along
the hedge and through another gap to a crossing farm track. Turn left
onto this and follow it, passing through a gate to Hayden Farm.

Continue straight on through the farm. Beyond the buildings, at
the end of a concrete road, turn right into a stony lane. Where it turns
left into a belt of trees, go straight on through the right-hand of two
gates and bear half right across a field, heading for a gateway at the
left-hand end of a group of trees in front of English Farm. Here turn
right into a stony lane and follow it, swinging left of the farm. Where it
enters a farmyard, bear left and turn right into another lane called
English Lane.

Just past a second entrance to the farmyard, turn left into another
stony lane. By a large house, cross a cattle grid and join a drive,

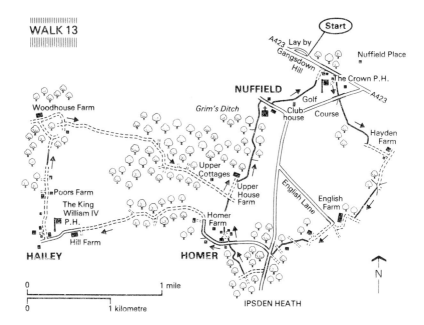

Start

A423 Lay by
Gangsdown Hill
Nuffield Place

The Crown P.H.

NUFFIELD
Golf
Club house
Course
A423

Grim's Ditch

Woodhouse Farm

Hayden Farm

Upper Cottages

Upper House Farm

English Lane

English Farm

Poors Farm

The King William IV P.H.

Homer Farm

Hill Farm

HAILEY

HOMER

N

0   1 mile
0   1 kilometre

IPSDEN HEATH

following it straight on to a left-hand bend by a telegraph pole. Here turn right over a stile and follow the fence of a copse on the right to its end. Bear left across the field to a stile into a lane. Cross this and then another stile, and bear half right across a field to a telegraph pole at the corner of a fence. Bear half left along the left-hand fence to a stile into a wood. Continue straight on through the wood, part of Ipsden Heath, crossing a track and eventually emerging on a road at Homer Turn.

Turn left along the major road, soon turning right into a stony lane called Ercot Lane. At the end of the right-hand fence, opposite a branching track to Harwood Lodge, turn right and follow a path along the inside edge of the wood to an old gate. Here bear half left through a belt of trees, then bear half right up a winding gulley path to a stile and gate into a lane at Homer.

Walkers wishing to take the shorter route should go straight on through a decrepit gate, passing the farmhouse to the right, and go through a gate between two garages. Follow the right-hand fence, passing through a gateway and eventually reaching a stile. Cross this and continue straight on, following the left-hand fence to a gate. Here ignore a crossing lane and go straight on up a lane towards Upper House Farm.

Walkers wishing to take the longer route should turn left into Homer Lane and follow it for $1\frac{1}{2}$ miles, ignoring all branching tracks. Where the drive to Fludger's Wood branches left, the surface of the lane changes from macadam to flint. It then passes through a wood after which the Berkshire Downs come into view. As you descend the escarpment, the Vale of the White Horse can also be seen ahead.

At Hailey, the surface reverts to macadam. Having passed the King William IV, turn right onto a wide track opposite the entrance to Paddock End and follow this for $\frac{1}{2}$ mile. Disregard a left-hand branch at Poors Farm, after which the track deteriorates to end at double gates. Continue straight on across a field to a stile by a cattle grid into a wood. Go straight on through the wood, ignoring all branching tracks, to Woodhouse Farm. Turn right here onto a rough road, following the edge of the wood. Where the road forks, fork left away from the wood and follow a track uphill. There are fine views behind. The track passes through a gate into a wood. Ignore all branching tracks in the wood. After leaving it, pass a pair of cottages, and where the track becomes macadamed turn left onto a track to Upper House Farm.

At this point, the long and the short routes are reunited.

At the farm, turn right over a stile before reaching the farmhouse. Follow a left-hand fence past the farmhouse, then bear half left across the corner of the field to a stile at the corner of a wood. Cross this stile and follow the path past a pit, then cross another stile and follow a right-hand hedge straight on to a gate into a belt of trees. Continue straight on through the trees to a stile onto the Ridgeway Path. Crossing Grim's Ditch, an ancient earthwork of uncertain origin, follow the path straight on, crossing two sets of wooden rails. Follow a right-hand hedge across a field to cross a stile onto a road at Nuffield.

Turn right here, passing the church, then turn left over a stile (still the Ridgeway Path) and bear half right across a field to a stile left of the golf clubhouse. Here bear half left through a belt of scrub and follow a path marked by a series of white posts across the golf course, again watching for golfers. Eventually you reach a lane leading out to the A423 near the Crown. Cross the road and retrace your steps to the layby.

Walk 14   Ewelme

3 or 7¼ miles (5 or 11.5 km)

Start: Recreation ground car park, Ewelme; O S map ref. 648912

Ewelme, today, is an idyllic sleepy Oxfordshire village with its
cottages and watercress beds nestling in the folds of the foothills of the
southern Chiltern escarpment. The village became prominent in the
early fifteenth century, when Chaucer's son married the heiress to the
manor. This prominence was furthered by their daughter's marriage
into the ill-fated Suffolk family. On the Suffolks' downfall, the manor
passed into the hands of the Crown resulting in the construction of
Ewelme Palace by Henry VII. During the course of the sixteenth
century, the palace was used by Henry VIII, whose bathing activities
led to the pool at the head of the stream (now a watercress bed) being
named King's Pool. The palace also served as a childhood home to
Princess Elizabeth, later Elizabeth I. After this period, however, the
manor was sold and the palace allowed to decay. Both walks are of
high scenic value, the longer one ascending the escarpment and
including the ancient hamlet of Swyncombe, the name of which
means 'valley of the wild boar'.

Ewelme, 2½ miles north-east of Wallingford, is signposted from the
A423 and B4009 roads. Starting from the car park by the recreation
ground at the south-eastern end of the village, take the lower road into
the village until you reach the primary school. This was built in 1437
by William and Alice Duke and Duchess of Suffolk, as a grammar
school, and is now the oldest primary school building in England. Just
past the school, turn half right onto a grass path which shortly joins a
macadam lane passing the almshouses and church, also built by
William and Alice around 1437. These are both worth visiting. The
almshouses were built around a quadrangle in brick and timber
(including some unusual herring-bone pattern brickwork) in a
fashion reminiscent of Oxford colleges. The church contains an
alabaster effigy of the founder's wife, Alice Chaucer, and brasses of
her parents, the son and daughter-in-law of the poet. Jerome K.
Jerome, author of *Three Men in a Boat*, is buried in the churchyard.

At the top of this lane, turn right onto a road and just past the
rectory on the left, fork left up a rough track which soon gives a view of
Ewelme Down and Ewelme Down House straight ahead. Follow this
track to a gate and stile where a view of Swyncombe Down opens up
ahead. Cross the stile and continue straight on, crossing another stile.
Bear slightly left to a third stile. Be sure to stop and look around you at
this point, where there are good views at all compass points including,

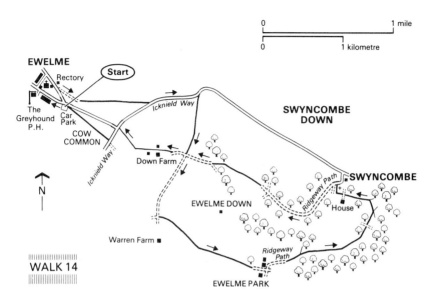

directly behind you, Wittenham Clumps, in ancient times a lookout post over the Thames opposite Dorchester.

From here, head for the top corner of an apparently triangular field on the side of Swyncombe Down, soon dropping down into Warren Bottom to join a road, the Icknield Way, an ancient Celtic road named after the Iceni. Continue straight on along this road over a small rise. At a left-hand bend, turn right through a gap beside a gate and follow a bridleway alongside a hedge for $\frac{1}{4}$ mile to another gate. Go through this gate and then follow the right-hand fence until you reach a macadam drive. Walkers wishing to take the short walk should turn right onto this drive and then read the last paragraph for the continuation.

Walkers wishing to take the longer walk should continue straight on across the drive onto a rough farm road. Follow this for $\frac{1}{2}$ mile until a track branches to the right a few yards before the farm road starts to climb past Warren Farm. Here turn left onto an ill-defined grassy track up the valley floor heading towards Ewelme Park House which can be seen on the skyline at the head of the valley. Around a slight bend in the valley a fence and a line of gates begin to mark the bridleway.

Where a hedge begins, keep left of this and follow it through a bridle gate and uphill to a gate near the top. Go straight on through this gate into a lane which soon gives a close view of Ewelme Park House to the right. There is an attractive pond hidden in bushes to the left.

At the far end of the garden wall, turn left between farm buildings onto the Ridgeway Path. At the far end of the farmyard, turn right along a lane until it opens into a field. Here continue straight on following the fence and a sporadic hedge until reaching the corner of a pine wood. Leaving the Ridgeway Path, cross a stile amongst the trees into Swyncombe Park and continue to follow the right-hand fence through several areas of woodland. Through the trees to the left Swyncombe House, an Elizabethan manor house extensively rebuilt in the last century, and the hamlet including the largely Saxon church of St Botolph may be glimpsed in places backed by Swyncombe Down.

On reaching a stile into the wood, the path enters the wood and continues just inside its edge. In Summer it may be preferable to continue outside the wood to another stile, thereby avoiding the nettle growth in the wood. At this second stile the routes reconverge. Inside the wood by this stile, bear slightly left crossing a metalled drive and soon reaching a clearing. At the far side of the clearing turn left through a kissing-gate and follow the edge of the wood downhill to another kissing-gate. Turn left again here and follow a depression in the ground across the park to a kissing-gate under some yew trees. Here follow a waymarked path through the trees and across a drive. Turn right through a gate into the churchyard of St Botolph's.

At the far side of the churchyard turn left, rejoining the Ridgeway Path, and bear slightly left through white gates into the tree-lined ancient road to Ewelme (now a bridleway). Follow this down the valley for $\frac{2}{3}$ mile past some magnificent chestnut trees, ignoring the Ridgeway Path branching left, until reaching a three-way fork. Here take the middle route. Leave the wood by a gate and continue straight on, following a hedge, until you reach another wood. Go through the bridle gate concealed in the bushes and follow the path through the trees to join a macadam drive which shortly crosses the outward route of the walk.

Where the drive bears left, bear right through a bridle-gate and head for a line of gates through Down Farm just left of a black building. Go through these gates and continue straight on, making for a treetop visible over the brow of the hill. On reaching this tree, at the corner of a hedge bear half right and follow the fence and hedge downhill through two gates to the Icknield Way road. Turn left onto this and pass two drive entrances. Then, opposite a green lane, turn right through a kissing-gate onto Cow Common and head slightly right of some distant buildings, gradually crossing the valley bottom to a kissing-gate by the car park.

Walk 15   Wallingford Bridge

5¼ miles (8.5 km)

Start: Wallingford Bridge (Wallingford end); O S map ref. 610895
In summer part of the route may be overgrown with nettles

Wallingford Bridge is a graceful structure built in 1809 on medieval
foundations on or near the site of the ancient ford from which Wallingford derives its name. It takes the Henley to Wallingford road
across the Thames and, in so doing, connects the town with the twin
villages of Crowmarsh Gifford and Newnham Murren. Wallingford,
which was granted its charter in 1155, claims to be the oldest royal
borough. With its narrow streets, a number of old inns and other
historic buildings, it is well worth exploring. North of the bridge are
the remains of Wallingford Castle, where Queen Matilda took refuge
after escaping from Stephen's men at Oxford. It was destroyed during
a siege in the Civil War. A number of earthworks marking earlier
fortifications can be seen in various parts of the town. Several interesting churches are also to be found, including St Peter's with its distinc-
tive spire, completed in 1777; St Leonard's, some way downriver, and
Crowmarsh Gifford Church, both of which are of Norman origin; and
St Mary's behind the Town Hall, with its four-pinnacled fifteenth-
century tower.

The walk includes a short section of towpath before visiting the
former hamlet of Mongewell, with its ruined Norman church, and
climbing into open country with panoramic views. The return route is
by way of Grim's Ditch, an exceptionally straight ancient earthwork.

Public car parks are available and signposted both in Wallingford
and at the Crowmarsh Gifford end of the bridge.

Starting from the Wallingford end of Wallingford Bridge, cross the
bridge and on reaching the far bank of the Thames, descend a flight of
steps on the left-hand side of the bridge onto the Thames Towpath.
Follow the path under the bridge and along the river bank for ½ mile.
After ¼ mile, St Leonard's Church is passed on the other bank and
eventually, about 120 yards, before the end of the towpath, a signpost
is reached pointing away from the river. Turn left here and follow a
worn path across the meadow to a footbridge by a gate, then continue
straight on to the next hedge. On reaching it, turn right and follow the
hedge. At Carmel College Farm continue straight on along a track
between the farm and a house, ignoring a branching track to the left.
Just past the farm, you pass Newnham Murren Church to the right, a
Norman church containing a long peephole of Norman origin and a
sixteenth-century brass with a bullet mark made in the Civil War.

51

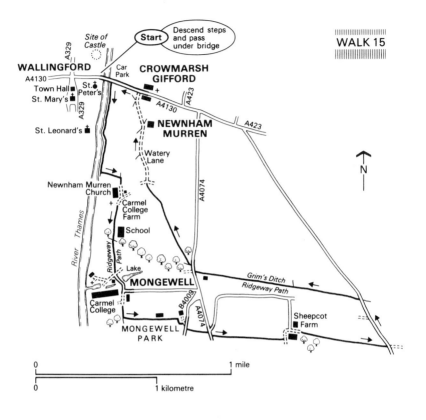

By the entrance to a school, the path becomes paved and enters Mongewell Park. Follow it straight on, until you reach a road. Here take a detour to visit Mongewell's ruined church, turning right along a drive into the grounds of Carmel College and then forking right along a drive signposted to the church. The church is hidden in trees to the left of a modern house and must once have been an attractive Norman building. The river can also be seen at this point, as well as some interesting examples of modern architecture amongst the college buildings.

Retrace your steps to the road, then turn right along it. Where it turns left, follow a school drive straight on. Where the drive turns right, leave it and go straight on through a gateway onto a fenced path. After less than 200 yards, by a large lime tree, turn left over a stile by a gate and follow a left-hand fence straight on across several fields to a drive. Do not enter this, but turn right along its fence to a stile. Cross this to emerge on the B4009 road.

Turn right here, then turn almost immediately left up a bank to a bridlegate. Now follow the left-hand hedge uphill to another bridlegate onto the A4074. Turn right here, then just past a copse to the left, turn left through the second of two adjacent gates and follow the left-hand fence to Sheepcot Farm. Just before the farm, turn left onto a farm road which, having passed the farmhouse, turns right. Disregard a road to the left and go straight on, passing a black barn to the left. Then fork left of a tree and follow the right-hand hedge, later a copse, straight on. Where the copse ends, go straight across the field and over a stile in a hedge gap. Now continue straight on for a further $\frac{1}{4}$ mile to a gate into a road called Cox's Lane. Turn left onto this and follow it to the top of a rise. Here turn left again onto a raised path through a line of bushes beside a deep ditch.

This is the ancient earthwork known as Grim's Ditch, the date and purpose of which have been an enigma to local historians for many years. It is thought to be some kind of boundary line or means of preventing livestock from straying, as its location is often not suitable for a defence line. Follow it straight on for nearly a mile to the A4074 opposite the entrance to Carmel College. Cross the road here, bearing slightly right to where the Ridgeway Path enters a belt of trees. Just inside this, fork right to a stile into a field. Cross this and go diagonally across the field, heading towards the tall spire of St Peter's Church. Then cross a stile and bear somewhat left of your previous course across the next field to a stile into a concrete farm road. Opposite the stile, go through a gate into a lane called Watery Lane. Follow this lane, disregarding all branching paths, for $\frac{1}{2}$ mile to the A4130 at Crowmarsh Gifford, a few yards east of Wallingford Bridge.

Walk 16   Goring-on-Thames

7½ miles (12 km)

Start: Goring & Streatley station forecourt; O S map ref. 602806

Goring-on-Thames, although in some ways resembling other Thames-side Chiltern towns, has a number of unique features arising from its geographical location. Situated in the Goring Gap which separates two ranges of chalk hills, the Chilterns and the Berkshire Downs, where these two ranges drop steeply into the Thames Valley, Goring has a scenically spectacular setting. This is enhanced by the wealth of trees on both sides of the river and a number of islands in the river itself. Goring is also of considerable historic interest as the point at which the ancient Icknield Way crossed the Thames well before Roman times. It can boast a substantially unaltered eleventh-century church built by Robert d'Oilly, containing a bell cast in 1290 and believed to be the oldest in Britain.

The walk, one of the finest in the Chilterns, follows the Thames for much of the way from Goring to Whitchurch, partly on the towpath and partly on an elevated terraced path through Hartslock Woods now a nature reserve. It returns over Whitchurch Hill before descending into Goring.

Goring, situated 8½ miles north-west of Reading, may be reached from the town by taking the A329 towards Wallingford and turning right at Streatley onto the B4009, crossing the Thames into Goring. Various small car parks are available, but on-street parking is inadvisable in the narrow streets of the town centre.

Starting from the railway station forecourt, follow the road northwards to a turning to the left over a railway bridge. Turn left here and then left again at the far end of the bridge. Follow this road, bending sharp right. Just past the Catherine Wheel, where the road turns right again, go straight on down Ferry Lane to the river. Turn left here onto the towpath and follow it for 1⅓ miles, passing under the railway bridge, until you reach Ferry Cottage, where the towpath transfers to the Berkshire bank.

At this point, at the time of writing, it is necessary to take a de facto path which is subject to alteration. Walkers are advised to heed any signs or waymarks. The de facto path turns left here between fences to a footbridge, then turns right. On reaching some wooden rails, turn left across a field to a stile into a fenced lane to return to the official route. Turn right here and follow this lane to its end.

At the end of the lane, climb through some rails and continue straight on to a further set of rails at the entrance to Hartslock Wood. Climb through these and continue straight on for ¾ mile, on a path

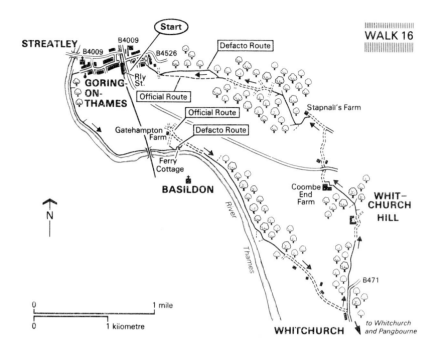

STREATLEY

B4009

B4009

B4526

Start

Defacto Route

GORING-
ON-
THAMES

Rly
St.

Official Route

Official Route

Defacto Route

Gatehampton
Farm

Ferry
Cottage

BASILDON

River

Thames

N

Stapnall's Farm

Coombe
End
Farm

WHIT-
CHURCH
HILL

B471

to Whitchurch
and Pangbourne

WHITCHURCH

0   1 mile

0   1 kilometre

which soon becomes a terrace cut into the side of a steep slope dropping into the Thames. Near the end of the woods, the path climbs
higher and swings away from the Thames. Ignore two branching
paths to the right and leave the wood by a gate. Follow a path between
a hedge and a fence, dropping steeply into a hollow, then climb
steeply to join a rough road. Continue straight on along this, ignoring
all side turnings for $\frac{3}{4}$ mile to join a road on the outskirts of
Whitchurch.

Whitchurch, and Pangbourne on the other side of the Thames are
both worth exploring, especially in view of their attractive setting by
the river. If wishing to explore these villages, turn right; otherwise
cross the road and turn left along a raised roadside pathway climbing
Whitchurch Hill. Where this pathway ends, cross the road again by
the war memorial and at a right-hand bend bear left off the road up a
sloping path to a gate. Go through this and continue straight on,
following the edge of a wood, until you reach a kissing-gate into a
fenced lane. Continue straight on along this lane and on reaching
Beech Farm, follow the track swinging right of the buildings. Now
cross a farm track, using two kissing-gates, and continue straight on
across a field with a fence to the left, aiming for a kissing-gate into a
wood. Follow an obvious path through the wood to a three-way fork.
Take the middle option, bearing half left across the wood to a stile into

55

a field. Go diagonally across the field, heading towards a barn ahead. Cross a stile and then continue to a gate into the farmyard. Enter this and by the corner of a building turn right through a gate into a field, and then turn left to a stile and gate into a lane at Coombe End.

Turn right along the lane, cross a rough macadam road and continue along another lane past some cottages. At the end of the lane, turn left onto a macadam road. Some 70 yards short of Stapnall's Farm, turn left through a gate and bear half right across a field to a gate in its corner into a lane. Turn left along this lane and on entering a wood, fork right through a gate, then fork right again and follow an obvious path for $\frac{1}{4}$ mile to another gate. Do not go through it, but turn left. In 50 yards, fork right. On emerging from the thick woodland, go straight on along a wide track, ignoring all branching tracks. After nearly $\frac{1}{2}$ mile, leave the woods by a stile. Follow the right-hand hedge to a second stile, then take another de facto path which bears half right, follows a hedge uphill, then turns left and later crosses a stile and drops (still following the hedge) to a track. At the track turn right over a stile, then immediately left over a wire fence. Bear half right across a field to a stile into a new estate. Follow its winding road to the main road, then turn left to return to the starting point.

4½ miles (7.5 km)

Start: King Charles Head, Goring Heath; O S map ref. 664789

Goring Heath is a collection of scattered dwellings rather than a village. The inn, the King Charles Head, derives its name from the tale that Charles I, while imprisoned in Caversham Park, was allowed to walk to the inn for a game of bowls.

Your walk takes you through quiet woods to the hamlet of Nuney Green, then turns towards the Thames, dropping down to the attractive and historically interesting hamlet of Mapledurham. From here, it returns running parallel with the river through Hardwick Park, finally climbing through woodland to Collins End and Goring Heath.

The King Charles Head at Goring Heath, the starting point of the walk, is situated 4½ miles north-west of Reading. It may be reached from the town by taking the A4155 across the Thames to Caversham, forking left onto the A4074 to the Pack Saddle at Chazey Heath and then turning left onto a winding lane to Trench Green and Goring Heath. Follow the lane for 2½ miles to the King Charles Head. There is a long stretch of wide, firm verge opposite the inn which is suitable for parking. Please do not use the car park next to the inn without the innkeeper's permission.

Starting from the King Charles Head, go westwards along the road. Near the end of a short section of woodland on the right, opposite a gate, turn right onto an obvious bridleway into the wood. Follow this through the woods for ½ mile, ignoring a crossing track after ¼ mile and two lesser paths branching left after crossing a dip. Eventually another track emerges from the left and by the drive to Fir Tree Kennels at Nuney Green you reach a bend in a narrow road. Turn left and follow the road to its end. Here turn right onto a rough stony track. At the end of the garden hedge to the right, turn right again onto a hedged path into a wood. Just inside the wood, disregard a path branching to the left and follow an obvious path straight on through the wood, fringed in Summer with foxgloves. After a while, a field becomes visible to the left and a stile is soon reached. Cross this and go straight on between a fence and a line of trees to a stile and gate leading into a road.

Cross this road, bearing slightly right, and take a farm drive almost opposite. You soon pass Whittle's Farm to the right; go straight on through a gateway. 100 yards further on the lane bears slightly left. Where the lane bears left again, turn right over a stile and follow the left-hand line of trees (soon becoming a copse) downhill to a gate and stile into a lane. Follow this lane downhill, crossing two more stiles,

57

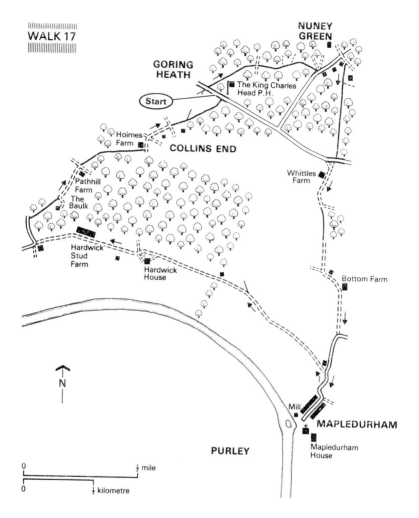

NUNEY GREEN

GORING HEATH

■ The King Charles Head P.H.

Start

Hoimes Farm

COLLINS END

Whittles Farm

Pathhill Farm

The Baulk

Hardwick Stud Farm

Hardwick House

Bottom Farm

N

Mill

MAPLEDURHAM

Mapledurham House

PURLEY

0   ½ mile

0   ½ kilometre

until you reach a stony lane in the valley bottom. Turn left onto this, passing Bottom Farm, where the lane becomes a concrete farm road. Follow the road for ¼ mile to a gateway onto the public road to Mapledurham. Turn right onto this road and follow it for ⅓ mile to its end by Mapledurham Church.

Mapledurham, the name of which is derived from the Saxon 'Mapledreham', meaning 'homestead by the maple tree', was until recently a very leafy and secluded hamlet, but the ravages of Dutch elm disease have drastically reduced its tree population. Along the village street are a number of seventeenth-century cottages, including a row of almshouses. At the far end of the village street, Mapledurham Mill, with its wooden tower, the oldest on the Thames, can be seen to the right. To the left is the church, built in about 1200 with the tower heightened in extensive renovations in 1862. An interesting feature of the otherwise Protestant church is a screened-off Catholic chapel belonging to the heirs of the Blount family, the traditionally Catholic owners of the Mapledurham Estate. Behind the church is Mapledurham House. The house was built by Sir Michael Blount in 1588 and made famous by John Galsworthy who names it as the home of Soames in part of his *Forsyte Saga*. Alexander Pope, the satirist, also visited it and befriended Martha Blount.

Retrace your steps along the road, until reaching The White House on the left. Turn left here into a fenced bridleway. After $\frac{1}{2}$ mile, ignore a branching path to the right and continue straight on, soon passing through a lodge gate into Hardwick Park. Throughout the length of the bridleway, there are fine views of the Thames Valley to the left and even in this park, despite a few trees, there are extensive views. After a further $\frac{1}{4}$ mile, ignore a left-hand branching track to Hardwick House and, on reaching a multiple junction, bear slightly left onto a macadam drive. Follow the drive for $\frac{1}{2}$ mile, passing Hardwick Stud Farm to the right, until you reach a lodge gate leading out to a bend in a road.

Here turn right onto the road. At a right-hand bend, opposite a gate and stile, turn right through a gap in the hedge into a wood and follow an obvious path uphill through the wood. On leaving the wood, the path joins a drive to a house called The Baulk and follows it straight on to a crossing lane by Pathhill Farm. Go straight on through a stile and gate here. Bear half right across a field to a stile in the hedge ahead. Having crossed this, continue straight on across the next field to the corner of a wood. Here bear slightly right, climbing across the field to a stile into a copse. Cross this and follow an obvious path through the copse to a squeeze-stile into another field. Continue straight on across this field to another squeeze-stile into a narrow path between a hedge and a fence. On emerging from this by Holmes's Farm, keep right of the farm buildings and then turn left into a rough lane past the front of the farm. Disregard a bridleway to the right sign-posted to Mapledurham and bear half right along a track across Collins End Green. Cross a macadam road and continue straight on along a fenced path to a squeeze-stile. Pass through this and follow the right-hand fence to an ordinary stile. Cross this, then bear half left across a paddock to a further stile opposite the King Charles Head.

Walk 18

Exlade Street

$4\frac{3}{4}$ miles (7.5 km)

Start: Exlade Street turn, A4074; O S map ref. 661813

Exlade Street is a tiny hamlet spread along an ancient main road from Reading to Wallingford which has been bypassed since the early 1970s. The existence of the hamlet is recorded in a document of 1241 and it boasts a number of ancient buildings including the Highwayman, dated 1625.

The walk passes through heavily-wooded countryside and visits Checkendon, a delightful village with one of the finest churches in the Chilterns, timbered cottages and a manor house with well-maintained formal gardens.

Exlade Street Turn, six miles north-west of Reading, may be reached from the town by taking the A4155 across Caversham Bridge into Caversham and turning left onto the A4074 towards Wallingford. After about five miles, the B4526 is passed turning left. Half a mile beyond this, look out for an unsignposted turning to the right leading to Exlade Street. Turn right here and find a suitable parking spot on the verge of this road.

Starting from the Exlade Street turn on the A4074, follow the Exlade Street road through the woods and on to the village. Pass the Highwayman, then after the first cottage on the right, turn right into a path between garden hedges. Follow it uphill to a gate and stile. Here turn right and follow the right-hand hedge to the corner of the field. Then turn left, continuing to follow the hedge to a stile in the top corner of the field which leads into a belt of trees. Go through this, then cross a wooden rail and turn left to a series of two stiles. Cross these and follow the left-hand hedge and fence to a point where the fence turns left. Here bear half right across the field, keeping left of a pit, to a stile in a double post-and-rail fence left of a cattle trough. Having crossed this, continue straight on across the next field to a stile to the right of an electricity pylon. Cross this and turn left into an old hedged lane. Follow this for $\frac{1}{4}$ mile to a road. Turn right onto the road and just past a large oak tree, turn left over or under a wooden rail at the beginning of a copse to your left, into a path between a fence and a hedge and line of trees. On reaching a stile in the fence, turn right through a gap in the hedge and trees to another stile, where Checkendon Court comes into view. Cross this stile and go straight on across parkland to a summer-house at the right-hand corner of the topiary hedge. Continue past this to a kissing-gate by a larger gate into a drive.

If wishing to explore Checkendon turn right along this drive and

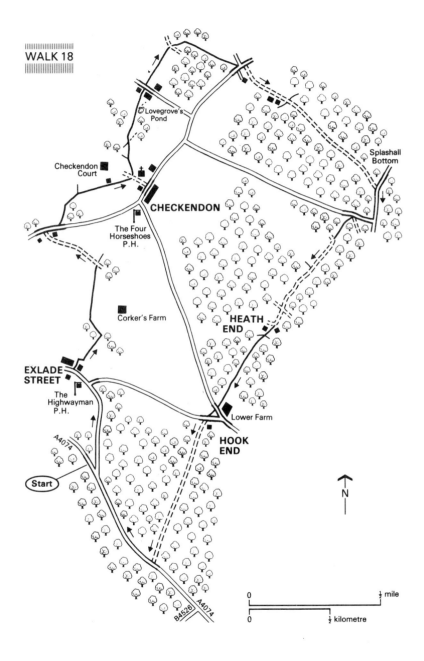

Lovegrove's Pond

Checkendon Court

CHECKENDON

The Four
Horseshoes
P.H.

Corker's Farm

Splashall
Bottom

**HEATH
END**

**EXLADE
STREET**

The
Highwayman
P.H.

A4074

Start

Lower Farm

**HOOK
END**

N

A4074

B4526 A4074

0   ½ mile

0   ½ kilometre

61

follow it to the village street, where the most attractive cottages, some of which must be Tudor, are situated. The twelfth-century church with its fifteenth-century tower and porch, which must surely rate as one of the finest and most lavish in the Chilterns, is to the left of the drive. It contains a rare, well-preserved thirteenth-century mural as well as a number of decorative tablets and brasses.

To continue the walk cross the drive, bearing slightly right to a gap by the corner of the churchyard wall, and turn sharp left onto a fenced path. On reaching a stile in the right-hand fence, cross this, then bear left across a field to a stile by a gate into a belt of trees. Go straight on across this tree belt, ignoring a crossing path. By a gate into a paddock, turn right and follow the paddock fence to a corner. Here continue straight on into the woods, soon reaching a large woodland pond, Lovegrove's Pond, to the right. At a fork by this pond, take the left-hand option and shortly leave the wood by a gate. Cross a paddock to a stile and gate by the corner of a hedge. Having crossed the stile, follow the left-hand hedge to a second stile. Then continue straight on through a small gate between the hedge and farm buildings to a road.

Continue straight on across the road through a narrow hedge gap to a stile. Cross the stile and follow a fenced path between paddocks to its end. Here cross the wooden rails and continue straight on across a field to a series of two stiles into some scrub, which lead you in a few yards to a track. Turn right onto this, going through a gate, then bear half left through a hedge gap into a field by the corner of a wood. Bear half right, following the outside edge of the wood to a gate leading out to a road junction. Here cross the major road to a point left of the junction, and take the left-hand of two rough tracks opposite. Follow a hedged, stony lane known as Judges Road past a farm, then on past a cottage and through woodland for $\frac{3}{4}$ mile to a quiet woodland road at Splashall Bottom.

Turn right onto this, and at a road junction turn right again. After about 130 yards, where a track merges with the road from the left, turn half left onto a path climbing through the wood. By the corner of a field, where the path merges with a bridleway from the right and widens, go straight on. Follow the edge of the field at first but later leave it behind. After over $\frac{1}{3}$ mile, two cottages are reached at the woodland hamlet of Heath End. Where the track turns right here, follow a path straight on between the cottages. Ignoring all crossing or branching paths, continue straight on for $\frac{1}{4}$ mile to a fenced path from the edge of the wood to a road at Hook End. Cross the road and go straight on across a green. Then cross another road, bearing slightly right, onto a hedged bridleway to the right of a house called Holly Shaw. Follow the bridleway straight on, soon entering a wood. Continue, ignoring all branching tracks, to a bridlegate. A few yards beyond this the A4074 road is reached. Turn right and follow the road back to the Exlade Street turn.

Walk 19   Highmoor Cross

5½ miles (9 km)

Start: The green near Highmoor Cross church; O S map ref. 700844

Highmoor, a combination of two hamlets ¼ mile apart, Highmoor Cross and Highmoor, is set in a heavily wooded location on the Reading to Nettlebed road in the heart of the Oxfordshire Chilterns. Like neighbouring Stoke Row, the village would seem to be of relatively recent origin, scattered along a road in a woodland clearing. This is suggested by the fact that both Highmoor and Stoke Row were, prior to 1952, only upland parts of some of the 'strip parishes' on the slopes from the Thames into the Chilterns – in Highmoor's case, Rotherfield Greys; in Stoke Row's, Ipsden, Mongewell and Newnham Murren. Both also have only had churches since Victorian times.

Much of the walk goes through woodland of various types interspersed with quiet pockets of farmland, mainly pasture. The larger village of Stoke Row with its oriental oddity, the Maharajah's Well, and its abundance of cherry trees is also visited.

Highmoor Cross, four miles west of Henley, may be reached from the town by taking the A423 westwards. Just before Nettlebed, turn left onto the B481 towards Reading. A quarter of a mile past the Old Dog and Duck, turn right into the turning signposted to Witheridge Hill, Stoke Row and Checkendon. Several gravel parking areas are available around the triangle of grass at this point.

Starting from the green near the church at Highmoor Cross, take the B481 northwards towards Nettlebed. Having passed the Old Dog and Duck, turn left into a driveway just before the bus stop on the left-hand side of the road and bear right between hedges to a stile. Cross this and follow the left-hand hedge to another stile into a wood. Just inside the wood, fork right through some holly bushes. At a junction by a telegraph pole, go straight on to a macadam drive. Continue straight on along this, disregarding two branches to the left, soon passing through a hedge and under two archways. Beyond these, the path continues straight on under a pergola and through two gates into another wood. Follow the obvious path straight on through the wood and over a stile into a field. Ignoring a second stile into the field to the right, follow the right-hand fence downhill to a stile into a further wood. Inside the wood, follow an ill-defined path bearing slightly right, until you reach a well-defined crossing path. Turn right onto this and follow it with a plantation to your left, until the path bears right, dropping down through some mature beech trees. Here turn left along a slight gulley which crosses the path, soon picking up a

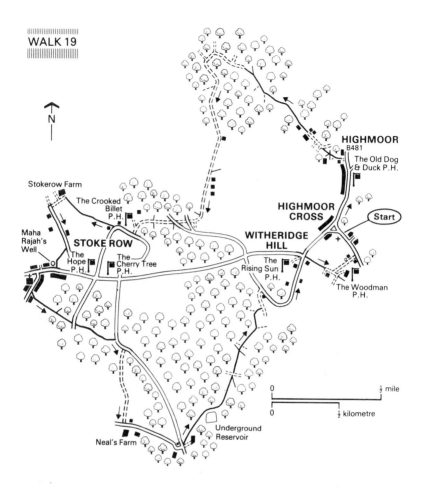

N

Stokerow Farm

The Crooked Billet P.H.

Maha Rajah's Well

STOKE ROW

The Hope P.H.

The Cherry Tree P.H.

HIGHMOOR
B481
The Old Dog & Duck P.H.

HIGHMOOR CROSS

Start

WITHERIDGE HILL

The Rising Sun P.H.

The Woodman P.H.

0 ½ mile

0 ½ kilometre

Underground Reservoir

Neal's Farm

more obvious path. Follow this, disregarding two branching tracks to the right, until you reach a rough lane at the edge of the wood.

Turn left onto this lane and follow it for ¾ mile, at first through the wood and later leaving the wood at a point by a cottage and continuing along a hedged lane, until entering a further wood. Where the track forks here, fork right and continue straight on, crossing two roads. Just beyond the second road, fork right up a track which climbs to join the drive to a house in a woodland clearing. Bear left onto the drive, soon reaching a road. Turn right onto the road, passing the Crooked Billet, and follow it to a sharp left-hand bend. Leave the road here by a kissing-gate on the right and follow a path between a hedge and a fence to a second kissing-gate. Go through this and continue beside the hedge through an orchard, until you reach a stile in the hedge. Cross this and continue along the other side of the hedge to two white gates. Go through these and follow the left-hand fence uphill to another white gate by Stokerow Farm. Turn left through this and follow a track straight on through three more gates to the end of a road. Turn left along the road and follow it for 350 yards, until you reach a narrow hedged path to the right with a white horse barrier across its end. Turn right onto the path and follow it out to the main road at Stoke Row.

The most interesting feature of Stoke Row is the Maharajah's Well with its oriental canopy, given by the Maharajah of Benares in 1864 as a token of thanks to Sir Edward Reade of Ipsden House for services rendered to his province.

Turn right along the road, almost immediately passing the Maharajah's Well to the right. Then, just before the church, turn left into School Lane. Just before the last pair of houses on the left, turn left again onto a fenced path leading into a wood. In the wood, bear slightly right and follow an obvious path until reaching a road. Cross this and continue straight on through the wood to a second road. Turn right onto this road, soon rounding a left-hand bend. After a few yards, turn right onto a stony track and follow the track through the wood and then between fields to a road at Neal's Farm. Turn left along this road and follow it, re-entering the woods and then re-emerging into a clearing where a road junction is reached by a few cottages.

Cross the major road here and at the beginning of the drive to a wooden bungalow opposite, turn left into the wood and follow a right-hand fence. After a while, pass an underground reservoir to the right. Now follow the obvious path, bearing left away from the fence, through a gate and past a plantation. Disregard both a track which emerges from the plantation and a wide crossing track; continue straight on, going through another gate into mature woodland. Where the path starts to descend, ignore a fork to the right and follow the path which curves first left and then right, until you reach a rough road at the edge of the wood. Turn left onto this. On reaching a macadam road by a cottage, turn right and follow the road which climbs and swings left to a road junction.

Turn right over a stile and follow a hedged alleyway uphill to another stile. Continue straight on across a field to a further stile which leads into a rough lane. Follow the lane straight on, turning left where it turns, and ignoring a stile ahead, follow the lane out to the B481 road. Your point of departure is 300 yards to the left.

Walk 20   Rotherfield Peppard

7¾ miles (12.5 km)

Start: Rotherfield Peppard primary school; O S map ref. 710816

Rotherfield Peppard, with its extensive common straddling the Reading to Nettlebed road, is rather a scattered community. Its houses are ranged about the common, the main group being in the area on the east side around the lane to the village church. Despite its proximity to the large residential sprawl of Sonning Common, a modern satellite of nearby Reading, the village has managed to preserve its rural charm and identity. As with many villages, its most interesting building is the twelfth-century church with its tower and steeple.

The walk, which passes the church and circles Sonning Common taking in Crowsley Park and Kidmore End with its picturesque village centre, traverses peaceful gently rolling hills and valleys, dropping down towards the Thames and some of the beechwoods which are the pride of the Chilterns.

Rotherfield Peppard, 5½ miles north of Reading, may be reached from the town by taking the A4155 road towards Henley across the Thames to Caversham, then forking left onto the B481 towards Nettlebed. Follow this for 4½ miles until you reach, at the top of a steep winding hill, a signpost to Peppard Church. Turn right here and look for a parking space, bearing in mind that for the sake of local residents and future visitors, it is advisable to avoid obstructing gateways or parking on mown frontages.

Starting from the Church of England primary school on the lane to the church, follow the lane eastwards to the church. Bear right of it and continue along a rough lane to its end. Here turn right, cross a stile and then turn left, passing a cottage and following a hedge. After a while bear right along a belt of trees to a New Zealand (barbed wire) gate. Go through this gate and follow a grassy track bearing right along the edge of a wood, then bearing left along a hedge to a barn and derelict cottage at Bottom Barn. Continue straight on along the track past the cottage and along a fence until you reach another New Zealand gate with a stile beside it. Turn right here, crossing the stile and immediately crossing another stile and a single strand of plain wire into a larch plantation. Follow an obvious path which soon turns sharp left into the midst of the plantation. After crossing a stile a barbed wire fence is reached. Turn left onto a path which follows this, climbing steeply until you emerge into a field. Continue straight on beside a hedge, and just before the end of the field go through a gap to the other side of the hedge.

66

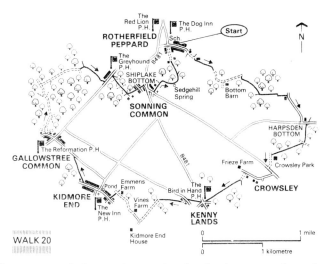

0   1 mile

0   1 kilometre

When you reach the new house ahead, take the narrow fenced path leading out to a macadam lane. Turn right onto this and follow it downhill to Harpsden Bottom. Here you reach another road by the attractive gabled Old Place, formerly Bottomhouse Farm. Turn left onto this road and after a few yards, turn right over a ladder stile into Crowsley Park. Walking at right angles to the road, make for a small marker post ahead. Having reached this, pass close to two small copper beeches and head for another marker post by a raised disused track. Here fork right and, passing two large cedars to your left, make for a stile by a group of large chestnut trees. Cross this stile and continue straight on to another stile at the left-hand end of an avenue of chestnut trees. Just beyond this Crowsley Park House, a red-brick Jacobean house, comes into view on the left. Continue straight on past the house to another stile leading onto a macadam drive. Turn left onto the drive and, ignoring two branches to the left, follow it to the lodge house and through the lodge gates to a road.

Turn left onto the road and follow it until you reach a turning on the right signposted to Crowsley. Take this turning and ignoring turnings to the left, follow the road past several cottages including a thatched cottage on the left-hand side. Just past this, turn left into a rough lane. At its end, fork half right onto a fenced path to the corner of a wood. Having rounded the corner, a stile is reached. Cross this and follow the right-hand fence, leaving it where it turns, and continue straight on to a pair of stiles in the next hedge. Continue straight on over the stiles and across the next field to cross another stile in the trees ahead. A few yards through the trees a road is reached. Turn right here and follow the road out to the Bird in Hand crossroads.

Go through a kissing-gate opposite into playing-fields and make for another kissing-gate by the furthest right of four holly clumps in the

67

hedge opposite. On reaching a road here, take a rough track to the right of the house opposite. Where the track ends, bear half right along a fenced path to some metal rails. Cross these and continue straight on across a field to a stile into a belt of trees. Inside the belt of trees a farm track begins. Follow this through the trees and then along a fence, until you reach a gate leading to a right-angle bend on a macadam lane. Kidmore End House can be seen ahead. Turn right into the lane and follow it past Vines Farm, where the macadam surface ends. Having passed Emmens Farm, an attractive gabled building on the right, turn left across a stile. Cross a field and go through an alleyway between gardens to a road at Kidmore End. Turn right along the road to the centre of the village.

The centre of Kidmore End with its pond, well, pub and early Victorian church clustered around a crossroads, is still a village of rural charm. Continue straight on here until, near the end of the village, you reach a chestnut tree on the left. Here turn right into the drive of a house called Norton Lee, and fork immediately left into a hedged path with a horse barrier. Follow the path which later crosses a field and enters a wood. Continue straight on here, until you join a road. Bear left onto this and follow it to a crossroads at Gallowstree Common.

Cross this crossroads and continue straight on. At a sharp left-hand bend by the corner of a wood, turn right into the wood. Just inside the wood, bear half left onto the centre track of a three-way fork, and at a further fork a few yards further on, bear half right. After some 200 yards, fork left by a tree with two trunks and follow a well-defined track, ignoring crossing tracks and lesser branches, until you reach a woodland pond near the corner of a field. Turn right here and follow an obvious track alongside a boundary ridge for nearly $\frac{1}{2}$ mile. Where the track forks right away from the ridge just past a large pit, continue to follow the ridge to a stile into a field. Cross this and follow a hedge. Where the hedge bears left, bear right across the field to the corner of a hedge by a new house. Follow this hedge to a road.

Turn left onto the road and on reaching a well, turn right into a wood. Here take the right-hand path, then at successive junctions, ignore a crossing track at the first, fork left at the second, ignore another crossing track at the third and fork left at the fourth, continuing until you reach the end of a wire-mesh fence. Just before this, turn left onto a path following the fence and ending in an alleyway out to a road. Cross this and continue up another alleyway climbing steps to a road. Turn right and cross a crossroads into Blounts Court Road. Just past a turning called Priory Copse, turn left onto a narrow hedged path leading into a wood. Ignore two branches to the left and follow the path to a bricked spring called Sedgehill Spring. Just past this turn left onto a path downhill. Near a New Zealand gate, fork left to a stile. Cross this and bear half left across a meadow to another stile. Having crossed this, follow a fenced path uphill through a plantation to a stile into a lane leading to Peppard Common.

Walk 21   Greys Green

4¼ miles (7 km)

Start: Greys Green village hall; O S map ref. 721829

Greys Green, with its cottages and blossom trees clustered around a village green, is the epitome of the idyllic English village. Strictly speaking however this hamlet forms only part of a scattered community collectively known by the parish name Rotherfield Greys, the church, pub, village hall and manor house being split between various hamlets.

This walk visits Rotherfield Greys proper, as well as taking in part of Grim's Ditch, some typical Chiltern beechwoods and rolling open landscape in the hills above Henley and the Thames Valley.

Greys Green, which is 2½ miles west of Henley, may be reached from the town by heading west from Henley Bridge up Hart Street, past the Town Hall, and following this winding road for three miles until reaching the open green of Greys Green. There is a gravel parking area in front of the wooden village hall on the left-hand side.

Starting from the village hall at Greys Green, cross the road and take the track round the back of the cricket green which leads to a farm. Just before the farm, turn right over a stile under a chestnut tree and follow the right-hand hedge to another stile leading into a wood. Cross the stile and follow an obvious path through the wood. Cross two more stiles before emerging into a field. Continue straight on downhill heading for the corner of another strip of woodland ahead. Follow the edge of this woodland to a stile leading into a road known as Rocky Lane. Cross the road here and take a path opposite which soon joins the macadam drive to Greys Court. Follow this straight on past Greys Court Farm and Greys Court itself, until you reach the little National Trust tollhouse.

Greys Court has had a chequered history. The medieval house, built by the de Grey family from which the name 'Greys' is derived, was fortified by the building of a surrounding wall in 1348. Four of the five towers and part of the wall still survive. The stables and a donkey wheel well-house remain from an Elizabethan house built by the Knollys family, but the house which stands here today is of late Stuart origin and in design resembles many large Oxfordshire houses.

By the tollgate fork half left and follow a fence through parkland, crossing two stiles, until you reach a track. Continue straight on along the track using a footbridge at the side, where it passes through a pond. Where the track turns left through a gate into farm buildings, cross the stile beside the gate and follow the fence to the right in which

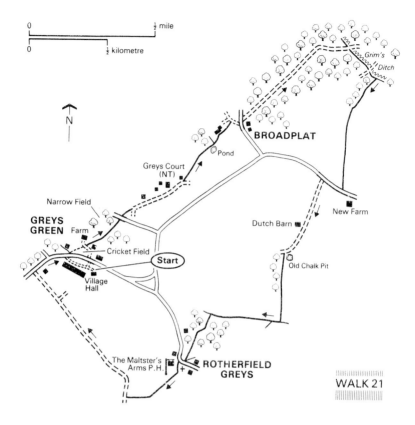

the stile is set. On reaching a stile, cross it and turn right onto a farm road leading to a road at the hamlet of Broadplat.

Turn left onto this road. At the end of the cottage garden opposite fork half right onto a waymarked path into Lambridge Wood. The path follows an old cart track but, as this is often waterlogged and overgrown by brambles, it is necessary to diverge slightly from this in places. After about ¼ mile, the path passes a field on the right. It then continues straight on away from the field, crosses a clear-felled area and reaches a crossing ridge and ditch, the ancient earthwork known as Grim's Ditch. Turn right here onto a waymarked path following the ditch. Ignore a path branching to the left and a crossing track. Now following the edge of the wood, look out for a stile on the right at the next hedge. Cross this and follow a line of trees and then a hedge to a stile. Having crossed this, bear slightly left and make for a stile and gate between a group of three trees and a telegraph pole to the right of New Farm.

Cross the stile and turn right onto a road. After a few yards, turn left

70

over a stile and follow a track past a Dutch barn until you reach an old chalk pit on the left. Just beyond the chalk pit turn left, crossing a metal gate and wooden rails, and follow a line of trees and later a fence downhill to a hedge in the valley. Turn right here, crossing a stile, and follow the hedge. Having crossed another stile, continue to follow the hedge until you reach a stile on your left into a wood. Cross this stile and follow a well-defined path uphill through the wood ignoring any branching paths. At the top of the hill, cross a stile and continue straight across a field to a kissing-gate at Rotherfield Greys.

The church opposite, built by the de Grey family in the thirteenth century, is noteworthy for a fine brass of Robert de Grey (d. 1387) in the chancel and the burial chapel of the Knollys family with its colourful tomb and monuments, added in 1605.

Turn right onto the road past the church, then turn left onto a path between the church and the Maltsters Arms. On crossing a stile, bear half right across a field to another stile. Having crossed this, bear half right again to a third stile leading into a hedged lane. Turn right onto this and follow it for $\frac{2}{3}$ mile. At the end of the lane, turn right onto a road which leads you back to Greys Green.

Walk 22   Henley-on-Thames (Marsh Lock)

7 miles (11 km)

Start: Mill Lane car park, near Marsh Lock; O S map ref. 771817

Marsh Lock, where the towpath traverses the weir stream by long wooden bridges above and below the weir, and with its steep wooded backcloth of Remenham Hill, is one of the most picturesque locks on the Thames. Although not starting at the lock itself, the walk returns by way of the towpath using the bridges to the lock. It also visits the hamlet of Harpsden, climbs gently onto a plateau at Upper Bolney, and explores various parts of Shiplake, including its church and lock.

The car park near Marsh Lock, from which the walk starts, may be reached from Henley-on-Thames by taking the A4155 towards Reading. On the outskirts of Henley, just past the Jolly Waterman, turn left into Mill Lane (signposted to the Sports Centre) and follow the road over a railway bridge to a car park on the left-hand side.

Starting from the car park in Mill Lane, turn right along the lane, crossing the railway bridge and returning to the A4155. Cross this and go straight on along Waterman's Road. Where the road turns right, continue straight on along a bridleway, passing between concrete posts. Follow the bridleway until you reach the Harpsden road at the entrance to Henley War Memorial Hospital. Turn left here and follow the road to Harpsden, ignoring a turning to the right, (Rotherfield Road) on the way. After leaving the built-up area, the road descends and Harpsden Court comes into view ahead.

Harpsden Court is, in part, thirteenth-century, but the majority of the present building dates from Tudor times. On rounding a sharp right-hand bend, the neighbouring twelfth-century village church comes into view and opposite this, a barn faced with old wooden blocks originally used in the manufacture of wallpaper. Having passed the church, turn left just before a road junction onto a path into the woods which, at first, runs parallel to Woodlands Road. Follow this gulley path uphill, ignoring the first fork to the right. At a second fork, bear right. Follow an obvious path, crossing a road and continuing straight on, until you join a stony track opposite a branching track to Harpsden Wood House and Harpsden Wood Cottage. Disregarding the latter branch bear left onto the track and follow it past a house entrance to a fork. Here take the right-hand option signposted to Pen-y-Bryn. Continue straight on, ignoring all crossing and branching tracks, until you reach a stile and gate ahead. Cross the stile and continue straight on across a field to a stile in the far corner. Cross the stile and another field to a further stile. Having

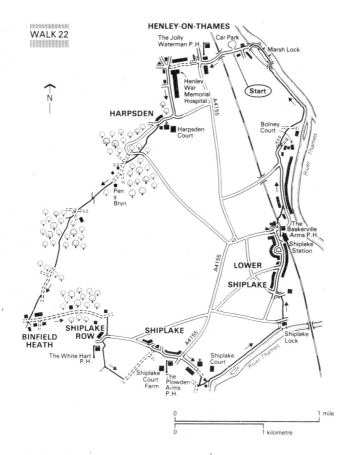

HENLEY-ON-THAMES

The Jolly
Waterman P.H.

Car Park

Marsh Lock

Start

Henley
War
Memorial
Hospital

A4155

Bolney
Court

River Thames

HARPSDEN

Harpsden
Court

Pen
y
Bryn

The
Baskerville
Arms P.H.

Shiplake
Station

LOWER

SHIPLAKE

A4155

SHIPLAKE
ROW

SHIPLAKE

A4155

BINFIELD
HEATH

Shiplake
Lock

The White Hart
P.H.

River Thames

Shiplake
Court
Farm

Shiplake
Court

The
Plowden
Arms
P.H.

0   1 mile

0   1 kilometre

crossed this, follow a left-hand hedge straight on to a stile into a lane
at Upper Bolney.

Turn right onto the lane and fork immediately left onto a track
towards a cottage. On reaching the edge of a wood, ignore a crossing
track and take a path straight on into the wood. Just inside the wood,
fork left and follow an obvious waymarked path through it to a stile
into a field. Continue straight on across the field, normally on a crop
break, to a track downhill through a small plantation. At the bottom
of the hill, leave the plantation by a stile and gate and, disregarding a
track to the right, continue straight on to a second stile and gate
leading into a lane. Follow this lane for about 200 yards, then pass
through a hedge gap into the next field. Here bear half right across the
field to a stile to the left of two modern houses. Cross this and follow an
alleyway between gardens out to a rough road, Kiln Lane, at Binfield
Heath.

Turn left into this lane and follow it for over $\frac{1}{2}$ mile, leaving Binfield Heath and passing through a wood. By a property called Kiln Land on the left, turn right through a gap in the hedge and follow a right-hand hedge to a gate leading out into a road. Cross the road and go through a gap in the hedge to the left of a gate by the White Hart, and follow the pub's boundary fence straight on to a corner. Here bear half left across the field, heading for a signpost near a single-pole electricity pylon. Turn left here and follow the right-hand side of the fence, until you reach a crossing farm track through a gateway in the fence. Turn left onto this track and follow it for $\frac{1}{4}$ mile, joining a concrete road and continuing straight on to a road at Shiplake. Here turn right and follow the road to the A4155 at the Plowden Arms crossroads. Cross this and continue straight on up a cul-de-sac lane to Shiplake church.

This church, built in about 1140 and enlarged in the thirteenth century, is best known as the church where the poet, Alfred Tennyson, married in June 1850. It also boasts a wealth of fifteenth-century French stained glass from the ruined Benedictine Abbey of St Bertin in St Omer. The glass was buried for safety during the French Revolution and later sold when the Order was suppressed.

By the church, go through a gate and bear half right down an alley bridleway. On emerging from this alleyway, turn left, ignoring tracks to the right, and continue down to the river. At the river bank, turn left onto the Thames towpath and follow the river for over $\frac{1}{2}$ mile to Shiplake Lock. Here cross a stile and turn left into a narrow lane beside a stone wall leading to a road. Turn right onto the road. After a few yards, turn left over a stile and follow the left-hand fence, crossing a second stile, until you reach a third stile by some trees. Bear half left over this stile and make for a further stile leading to a raised road. Turn left onto this road subsequently crossing a bridge. At a road junction, turn right and follow the road for nearly $\frac{1}{2}$ mile to the Baskerville Arms crossroads at Lower Shiplake. Here bear half right into a cul-de-sac, passing Shiplake Post Office. At the end of the road go straight on along an alleyway between a hedge and a fence to a railway crossing with stiles on each side. Beyond this, go straight on through a kissing-gate and along a further alleyway to a road. Turn left along this and follow it to its end, disregarding a turning to the left and passing the entrance to Bolney Court.

Here go through a white gate to the left of the entrance to Fairacres and follow a fenced path between two private roads, until you reach a kissing-gate into the left-hand road, now a grassy track. Follow this track for a few yards, then, by a tree, fork half left onto a fenced path to a stile and footbridge. Having crossed these, continue straight on to the river bank at the site of the former Bolney Ferry. Now turn left along the Thames towpath and follow it to Marsh Lock. Here go through a gate, then over a long footbridge to the lockside and back over another long footbridge to the Oxfordshire bank. On reaching this, take the road straight on back to the car park.

Walk 23   Henley-on-Thames

7¼ miles (11.5 km)

Start: Kings Road car park; O S map ref. 759829

Henley-on-Thames, home of the famous Royal Regatta, has, for the
last century or more, been a fashionable riverside resort. Although
this has, to some extent, contributed to the architectural beauty of the
town, its former role as a commercial centre is responsible for much of
its legacy of picturesque buildings. Prior to the age of railways, the
town was of considerable commercial importance, being both a river
port and a bridgehead on a main road crossing the Thames. In Hart
Street are to be found a number of ancient timber-framed houses and
inns. The Town Hall, around which the street divides, was built in
1796 on the site of the medieval Guildhall, and the imposing Parish
Church and nearby almshouses date from the fourteenth to sixteenth
centuries. Henley Bridge, one of the most graceful on the Thames,
was built in 1786 to replace a wooden structure swept away by a flood
in 1774.

The walk starts near the centre of the town and follows the Regatta
course past Fawley Court and Temple Island to Greenlands, then
climbs through woodland to the remote heights of Fawley,. returning
by way of the commanding Henley Park ridge.

The large municipal car park in Kings Road, from which the walk
starts, is signposted from most approaches to the town.

Starting from the northern entrance to Kings Road municipal car
park, turn right into Kings Road and follow it. winding downhill to its
end. Cross the main road here and turn left, forking right at the
roundabout onto the A4155 towards Marlow. After passing the drive
to Phyllis Court, at a right-hand bend, turn right through a kissing-
gate. Follow the path signposted to Hambleden along the right-hand
fence to a kissing-gate near the river. Go through this, then turn left
along the river bank. Follow the Thames closely for more than a mile.
After just over ½ mile, Fawley Court, a mansion built for William
Freeman to a design by Sir Christopher Wren in the late 1680s, can be
seen to the left from one of the many footbridges on this path. Further
on is Temple Island, so named because of the small temple on its
southern tip; it is the starting point of the Regatta course.

Near the far end of the island, the path begins to bear away from the
river and crosses two footbridges in a belt of trees. Continue straight
on across the next field to a further footbridge left of a large chestnut
tree surrounded by smaller poplars. From here, the path continues
straight on, crossing the macadam drive to Greenlands. 150 yards
further on, a stile leads out onto the A4155 road. Turn right along the

75

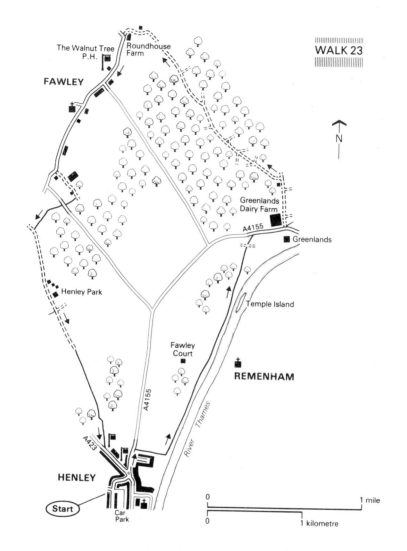

The Walnut Tree P.H.
Roundhouse Farm

FAWLEY

Greenlands Dairy Farm

A4155

Greenlands

Henley Park

Temple Island

Fawley Court

A4155

REMENHAM

River Thames

A423

HENLEY

Start

Car Park

0   1 mile

0   1 kilometre

road. Where the pavement ends, cross the road carefully and take a farm road opposite, passing Greenlands Dairy Farm. Follow the farm road for $\frac{1}{4}$ mile. At an old gateway just past some red-brick cottages, turn left into a fenced track, bearing half right where it opens out into a field.

Enter the wood by a gate and, disregarding all branching and crossing tracks or paths, follow a waymarked track through it, going straight on except at a point about $\frac{1}{2}$ mile into the wood, some distance after going through a gateway. Here the track twists to the left and the concealed waymark may be missed. After nearly a mile, during which the path has climbed to about 500 feet above sea-level the track re-emerges from the wood and continues as a lane between a fence and a hedge. The lane emerges on a road by Roundhouse Farm at the scattered community of Fawley.

Turn left onto the road and follow it for a mile passing the Walnut Tree, a road to the left, a road to the right and Fawley Church, hidden in trees. This twelfth-century church with a later tower and chancel contains some ornate Jacobean woodwork as well as a marble monument with alabaster effigies of Sir James Whitelocke and his wife, parents of the judge who refused to pass judgement on Charles I. The churchyard also contains two large mausoleums containing the remains of the Freeman and Mackenzie families who, for centuries, owned Fawley Court.

At a sharp right-hand bend, where a chestnut tree, a fire hydrant and a footpath sign are clustered together on a triangle of grass to the left, turn left into a rough lane. On emerging by a paddock to your right, turn right over a stile into a narrow path between a hedge and a fence. Follow this to a stile into a wood. Cross the stile and continue straight on downhill to a road. Cross the road, bear slightly right over a stile and follow the outside edge of the wood, crossing two more stiles, until the edge of the wood bears away to the left. Here, continue straight on following the right-hand field boundary to a further stile leading into a stony lane. Turn left here and follow the lane for $\frac{1}{2}$ mile, passing Henley Park House. Where the lane (now a macadam private road) turns sharp left, go straight on through a kissing-gate and follow a grassy track across open parkland. By a farm shed, go through another kissing-gate and continue straight on until you eventually drop down to a kissing-gate into a wood. Follow an obvious path downhill through the wood. On leaving the wood, the path becomes enclosed between a hedge and a fence and continues to the A423 road. Turn left along this and follow it to a roundabout, from which you retrace your steps to Kings Road car park.

Walk 24   Medmenham

7 miles (11 km)

Start: Ferry Lane, Medmenham; O S map ref. 805845
In summer parts of the route may be overgrown with nettles

Medmenham, a Thames-side village on the Marlow to Henley road
barely noticed by the passing motorist, is both attractive and rich in
history. The riverside abbey at the bottom of Ferry Lane was
originally built by the Cistercian order in the twelfth century, but was
already ruinous at the time of the Dissolution. Skilfully rebuilt by Sir
Francis Dashwood in 1745, it was used by his 'Knights of St Francis',
otherwise erroneously called the 'Hellfire Club', for reputedly
orgiastic activities. Further extensive renovations took place in 1898.
Amongst other interesting features, the village has a twelfth-century
church with a fifteenth-century tower, a sixteenth-century inn, an
Iron Age hill fort on the hilltop east of Bockmer Lane and a number of
manor houses in the vicinity.

The walk takes you through remote heavily-wooded countryside
via the hamlets of Bockmer End and Rotten Row, as well as the
possible lost hamlet of Holywick, to the village of Hambleden. The
return is by a direct route with fine views of the Thames and
Hambleden valleys.

Medmenham, three miles south-west of Marlow, may be reached
from the town by taking the A4155 towards Henley, until you reach
the village. At the village crossroads, turn left into Ferry Lane, where
cars can be parked at convenient points on the roadside. Care should
be taken not to block entrances or park on mown verges.

Starting from the entrance to Ferry Lane at Medmenham
Crossroads, cross the A4155 into Bockmer Lane and fork half right off
the road up a terraced footpath. As you climb, ignore a path forking
left and a crossing track at the hilltop which follows the line of the Iron
Age fortification. Continue straight on along an ill-defined path
between pits, until you reach a kissing-gate. Go through this, then
turn left along a track. At a junction of tracks, continue straight on
through another kissing-gate, following a fence to a road opposite the
front door of a house. Turn right along this road, ignoring all
branching drives. Where the public road ends, continue straight on
along a private road (and public footpath) towards The Hermitage.
On reaching its gateway, fork left onto a well-defined path and follow
this downhill. The path becomes a drive by Pheasantry Cottage. On
reaching a junction, turn right.

At the edge of a wood by a telegraph pole, turn left on a path uphill
into a wood. On reaching a crossing path, turn left along it, passing

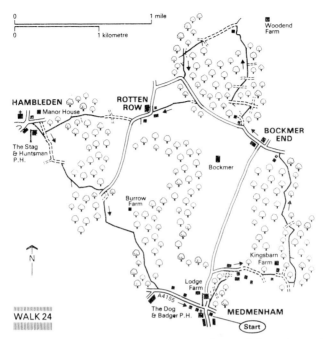

under a yew tree to a stile. Having crossed this, follow the path for more than $\frac{1}{3}$ mile, crossing another stile at one point, until you eventually leave the wood by a stile. Cross a farm track and a second stile and follow a right-hand fence uphill to a stile into another wood. Inside the wood, bear right and follow a well-defined waymarked path through it, eventually emerging at a stile. Cross this and bear half right across a field to a stile just right of some cottages. Having crossed this, turn right and follow a path between a hedge and a fence to a road at Bockmer End.

Turn left along this road and follow it for $\frac{1}{3}$ mile, disregarding branching roads to right and left and passing through the hamlet with its attractive old cottages. Just before Flint Cottage on the right, turn right onto a track. Where the track turns left into dog racing kennels, go straight on and enter a wood. Inside the wood, fork half right over a stile and, ignoring a branching path to the right, follow the path downhill through a plantation. At the bottom of the hill, turn left into a wide fire break. After about 250 yards, turn right onto a concealed path. Follow it uphill, ignoring two crossing tracks and a right-hand branching track, to a stile at the edge of the wood. Cross this and follow a left-hand hedge through two fields, passing a pit, to some ruined farm buildings at Holywick. Old documents refer to a chapel having been here and this would suggest that Holywick may be the site of a lost hamlet.

Just past the farm buildings, turn left onto a grassy track and follow it beside a left-hand hedge into a valley. At the valley bottom, go straight on into the corner of a wood, bearing slightly left into the wood, then forking right and following its inside edge uphill. Eventually the edge of the wood is left behind. At a five-way junction, ignore the first left-hand path and turn left onto the second, following an obvious path through the wood to a road. Turn left along this. After 300 yards, turn right over a stile by a gate and at the edge of the wood, cross a stile by a New Zealand (barbed wire) gate. Continue straight on across a field, with views to the left towards Bockmer House and Berkshire, to a wooden rail and stile under a tree to the right of a farm ahead. Having crossed these, follow a left-hand fence, crossing two more stiles, into a farm drive. The drive leads to a road at the hamlet of Rotten Row.

Continue straight on along the road. At a left-hand bend, go straight on through a gate and follow a grassy track to a gate and stile. Cross the stile and a crossing track and follow the grassy track across one more field. Here follow a crop break straight on to the corner of a wood. Follow the edge of the wood straight on to a stile into it, then follow a waymarked path downhill through the wood, disregarding a crossing path. On emerging at the corner of a field, a fine view opens out along the Hambleden and Thames valleys towards Henley. Continue straight on between a fence and the edge of the wood. On reaching a lane, if you wish to visit Hambleden, either go through a kissing-gate opposite and bear half right across a sports field or turn right along the lane.

Hambleden, birthplace of Lord Cardigan, who led the Charge of the Light Brigade in the Crimean War, is well worth a visit. At times, an attractive bourne flows through the village which boasts many fine brick-and-flint cottages and quaint little shops. Its extensively renovated fourteenth-century church has retained several fine monuments. The bookseller, W. H. Smith, the first Viscount Hambleden, is buried in the churchyard and his descendants still live in the nearby manor house.

To continue the walk, turn left along the lane. At a junction turn left again, then soon turn right over a stile and follow a right-hand hedge, which gradually peters out, to a stile into a wood. Inside the wood, ignore a stile to the right and follow an obvious path along the edge of a thicket. Then bear half left through mature beechwood, following a waymarked path to a road. Cross this, bearing half right, cross a stile and bear half left into a gulley, ignoring a branching path to the right. At the edge of the wood, turn right and follow a left-hand fence. After some 300 yards, follow a fenced path across two fields, with the partly sixteenth-century Burrow Farm to the left, into another wood. Inside the wood, bear right and follow a well-defined path for nearly $\frac{1}{2}$ mile, eventually dropping to a stile at the A4155 road. Turn left along this and follow it back to Medmenham.

Walk 25   Bovingdon Green (Bucks)

4¾miles (7.5 km)

Start: Bovingdon Green village green; O S map ref. 833870

Bovingdon Green, on a hilltop above Marlow, is a pleasant hamlet with most of its cottages clustered around a village green. The walk takes you through the thinly populated and heavily-wooded hill country west of Marlow with fine views across the Thames Valley and the surrounding hilltops and deep ravine-like valleys.

Bovingdon Green, one mile west of Marlow, may be reached from the town centre by heading west along West Street (A4155) and turning right into Quoiting Square leading to Oxford Road. Follow the road towards Frieth for one mile to Bovingdon Green, where the village green opens out to the left at a road junction. Cars can be parked at various spots around the green, but should not obstruct tracks or entrances.

Starting from the west corner (or back right-hand corner as seen from the road junction) of the green at Bovingdon Green take a stony lane leaving the corner of the green. After a few yards, turn left over a stile. Follow a narrow path between a hedge and a fence, soon turning right and then continuing straight on, until you reach a stile in the hedge. Cross this and continue along the other side of the hedge to a stile and gate into a wood. Cross the stile and follow the right-hand fence through the wood, passing a pit and ignoring a stile in the fence. Continue straight on, leaving the wood and climbing to a gate. Go through this and follow a grassy track across a field to Hook's Farm. By the farmhouse, turn right into the farmyard, then turn left and follow a macadam farm road out to another road. Cross this and go straight on along a farm track beside a left-hand hedge. Follow the track, bearing half left across a field to a gate onto the A4155 road.

Turn right along this busy main road and just inside a wood, before reaching a cottage to the left, turn right over a concealed stile into the wood. Some way into the wood, ignore a branching path to the left and continue straight on. The path soon becomes better defined and joins a track by the corner of a field. Bear slightly right onto this and follow it out to a road junction. Cross the major road here and fork half left over a boundary ditch and ridge marking the parish boundary of Medmenham and Great Marlow. Having crossed these, turn right and follow them for ¼ mile, until reaching a major crossing track, where the ditch rejoins the road. Here turn left and follow a way-marked, if ill-defined, path downhill to a stile into the corner of a field.

Leaving the woods behind for the present, cross this stile and follow a right-hand hedge straight on for ¼ mile. Where the hedge turns left,

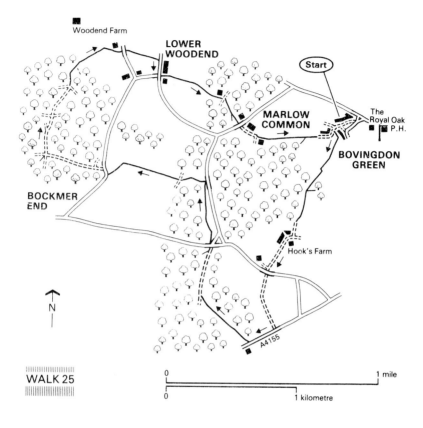

Woodend Farm

LOWER WOODEND

Start

MARLOW COMMON

The Royal Oak P.H.

BOVINGDON GREEN

BOCKMER END

Hook's Farm

N

A4155

WALK 25

0   1 mile

0   1 kilometre

cross a stile in it and follow the other side of the hedge to a gate and stile into a road. Here turn right onto the road and follow it downhill. Just before a right-hand bend, turn left over a stile into a wood and follow a wide track along the valley bottom,. going straight on where the main track turns right. After $\frac{1}{4}$ mile, where the deciduous plantation to the right gives way to a coniferous one, turn right onto a wide track between them. Where this forks, bear half right and follow a climbing track which gradually narrows, disregarding a crossing track. Eventually you emerge at the junction of several tracks by the gateway to a forestry compound at the top of the hill. Here cross a stile into the compound, then bear half right, following a narrow path downhill. At the bottom, ignore a right-hand branching path, and climb to a series of two stiles leading into a field. Cross these and follow the right-hand hedge across the field and over a stile; then continue straight on beside the hedge. At a corner in the hedge, bear half right across the field to where the garden fence of a cottage joins the hedge. Here cross a stile in the hedge and follow the other side of the hedge to a stile into a road. Cross the road and a stile opposite, then bear half right across a field, heading for a stile near the left-hand end of a long building in the tiny hamlet of Lower Woodend.

Cross this stile and turn right onto a road. At a road junction turn left into a driveway, passing the corner of a house, and follow a path between a hedge and a fence and over two stiles into a field. Follow the left-hand hedge downhill to a stile at the bottom. Cross this and climb steeply uphill, bearing slightly right, to a stile into the wood at the top. Inside the wood, follow a path between a wall and a fence to a stony track. Cross the track bearing slightly left, then bear half right across wooded Marlow Common, ignoring crossing tracks and keeping left at a fork, until you reach another road opposite the drive to Wolmer Wood. Take this drive and where it turns right by a telegraph pole, leave the drive and follow a fenced path straight on into a wood. At the far side of the wood, cross a stile and continue straight on across a field to another stile. Cross this stile and continue straight on across the next field to a gateway. Go through this and follow the left-hand fence to a stile and gate into a lane which leads you back to Bovingdon Green.

Walk 26   Bourne End

7¾ miles (12.5 km)

Start: Bourne End public library car park; O S map ref. 894875

Bourne End is near the confluence of the River Thames and the Wye, which runs through High Wycombe. Although its existence was recorded in the thirteenth century, it has developed from a hamlet into a small town only in relatively modern times. Its principal attraction today is the river. The walk follows the Thames towpath along the beautiful stretch of river between Bourne End and the Marlow Bypass, against the magnificent backdrop of Winter Hill. The route then crosses the river and climbs through Quarry Wood to the ridge of Winter Hill before dropping down and crossing Cock Marsh to the Berkshire towpath and the picturesque village of Cookham. From here the walk returns via Cookham Bridge to Bourne End.

Bourne End, four miles north of Maidenhead, may be reached from the town by the A4094. In Bourne End, fork left onto the A4155 to the Shopping Parade, where a free car park is signposted to the right.

Starting from the car park by Bourne End Public Library, follow the car park drive out to the Shopping Parade. Here cross the main road and take Wharf Lane opposite, bearing right, and follow it to a road junction with a small traffic island with a tree on it. Bear slightly left here, crossing the railway and entering a boatyard to reach the Thames towpath. Turn right onto this and follow it along the river bank until you leave the built-up area at a small car park at Spade Oak Wharf, site of a former ferry. Cross the car park and follow the towpath for a further two miles.

Eventually Marlow Bypass Bridge is reached. At the time of writing, Bucks County Council plans to arrange for the building of a flight of steps to the bridge from the towpath. Turn right here and climb these steps, then follow the Bypass over the river with views to the right of the picturesque riverside town of Marlow. On crossing a further bridge over Quarry Wood Road, some 200 yards beyond the river, turn left onto a flight of steps and descend to this road. Turn right along the road and follow it until it crosses a bridge over a stream into Quarry Wood. At a road junction here, leave the road and continue straight on along a woodland path, soon bearing left and climbing gently up a terraced path across the face of the hill. Near the top, the path bears right and climbs more steeply to a road. Do not join the road, but bear left onto another terraced footpath following the contours of the hill. In places, extensive views open out through the trees across Marlow and the Thames Valley to the hills above High

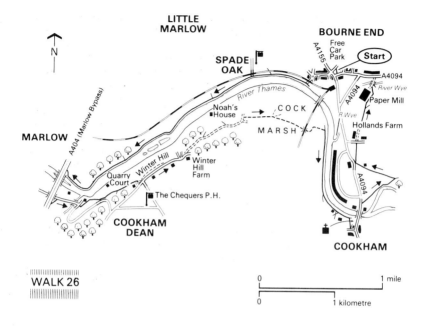

LITTLE
MARLOW

BOURNE END

SPADE
OAK

Start

Free
Car
Park

A4155

A4094

River Wye

A4094

Paper Mill

River Thames

Noah's
House

COCK

MARSH

R.Wye

Hollands Farm

MARLOW

A404 (Marlow Bypass)

Winter Hill

Winter
Hill
Farm

Quarry
Court

A4094

The Chequers P.H.

COOKHAM
DEAN

COOKHAM

N

WALK 26

0   1 mile

0   1 kilometre

Wycombe. Ignore a branching path to the right and after $\frac{1}{3}$ mile, join a drive out to a road.

Turn left onto the road, and at a road junction leave the road and follow the grassy hilltop of Winter Hill, until bushes and nettles force you back onto the road. Disregard a road junction and, by Winterhill Farm, turn left onto a track. Follow this downhill, ignoring lesser branching tracks, to Cock Marsh. Here follow the track, turning left to a gate, but do not go through this gate. Instead turn right and follow a fence and hawthorn hedge along the edge of the marsh, a National Trust property. Where the hedge and fence turn left, bear half right across the marsh to a bridge under the Bourne End railway near two double-pole electricity pylons. Go under the bridge, crossing a stile at each side, then bear left for a few yards to avoid a drainage channel. As soon as possible bear right to continue across the marsh to join the Thames towpath. Turn right onto this and follow it for $\frac{3}{4}$ mile, passing through three gates to Cookham.

At the third gate, by a boatyard, the path becomes macadam and passes a riverside green. At the far end of this, turn right onto a path through a gate into the churchyard, passing the twelfth-century church to the left and continuing out through another gate to the busy but narrow A4094. The village centre is to the right and is well worth a visit. Otherwise turn left and follow the A4094 over Cookham Bridge.

After passing a boatyard to the right, turn right through a kissing-gate. Bear half left across a field to a squeeze-stile near a bend in one of the four streams into which the Thames temporarily divides below Cookham Bridge. Go through this and follow the river bank for a short distance. At the next field boundary, turn left and follow the edge of the field to a footbridge. Do not cross this, but turn sharp left, heading back across the field to a gate. Go through this and follow the right-hand hedge, swinging left and then right around a small compound to a kissing-gate in the corner of the field, leading to a road.

Turn right onto the road, then immediately right again through another kissing-gate into the next field. Bear half left across this, keeping left of a cattle drive, to a kissing-gate into another road. Cross this and continue straight on along a farm road past Hollands Farm. At the end of the road go through a kissing-gate and follow the left-hand hedge to a second kissing-gate. Here continue straight on, through the gate joining a raised concrete path beside the paper mill fence. At the end of the field, enter an alleyway which eventually merges with the mill drive. Continue straight on along the drive to the A4094, then turn left along this road. Where the A4094 turns left, go straight on and just before Lloyds Bank, turn right along a footpath back to your point of departure.

Walk 27   Wooburn Green

$6\frac{1}{2}$ miles (10.5 km)

Start: Wooburn Green car park; O S map ref. 913885
In summer parts of the route may be overgrown with nettles; many
places are boggy due to poor drainage.

_____

Wooburn Green, although now linked by continuous development to
High Wycombe, has managed to preserve some of its village
character. Set around a well-kept village green, it has a number of
attractive old cottages. The River Wye, with its pollarded willows,
flows past the village and there are green hills on both sides of the
valley.

The walk itself crosses the Wye and scales the ridge to the east,
makes a wide circle on the surprisingly remote hilltop plateau taking
in the hamlets of Burghers Hill and Littleworth Common and a
variety of pleasant countryside in between, and then drops back down
into Wooburn Green.

Wooburn Green, $2\frac{1}{4}$ miles southwest of Beaconsfield, may be
reached from High Wycombe by taking the A40 eastwards for $2\frac{1}{2}$
miles and then turning right onto the A4094; or by leaving the M40 at
Junction 3 (Wycombe East), taking the A40 westwards for $\frac{1}{4}$ mile and
then turning left onto the A4094. Follow this for nearly two miles to a
large village green on the left, then turn right onto a road signposted to
Flackwell Heath, to a free car park on the right before the railway
bridge. (This is not to be confused with the Red Lion car
park.)   Starting from the entrance to the public car park at Wooburn
Green, turn left down Whitepit Lane to the A4094. Cross this and go
straight across the green onto Windsor Hill, a road leaving the green
on the far side. Follow the road out of the village, crossing the River
Wye by a narrow humpbacked bridge. At a sharp right-hand bend,
turn left up some steps onto a footpath to a stile. Cross this and bear
right, following the hedge uphill, until you go through a gap into some
woodland. Here continue parallel to the road but do not join it until
reaching a road junction at the top of the hill. Turn right here, crossing the top of the hill road, and entering a bridleway between a fence
and a hedge to the left of the entrance to a private road called The
Chase. Follow this bridleway straight on, eventually crossing The
Chase and passing between buildings into the end of the village street
at Burghers Hill.

Follow this narrow road through the hamlet to a sharp left-hand
bend. Turn right here passing a gabled cottage whose upper storey
juts out across this bridleway in a fashion most perilous to

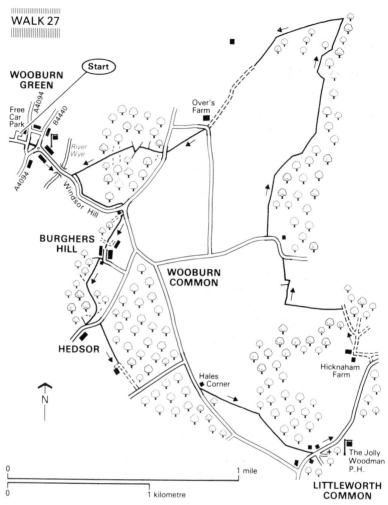

horseriders! Just beyond this, turn left and follow the fenced bridleway along the edge of a wood. After some 200 yards, ignoring a right-hand branching path, bear half left into the wood. Ignoring two branches to the left and then two to the right, follow the bridleway to a bridlegate into a road near Hedsor Rectory. Turn left along the road. At a left-hand bend, turn right into a bridleway between a hedge and the edge of a wood. After $\frac{1}{4}$ mile, by a cottage, the bridleway joins a drive and follows it out to a road. Turn left along the road to a junction, then turn right along another road. Just past a cottage at a left-hand bend, a path branches left between the garden hedge and a wood. Take this and on leaving the wood by a stile, continue straight on beside a hedge. After $\frac{1}{4}$ mile, two stiles lead you into a fenced path beside a wood. In $\frac{1}{3}$ mile along this path you reach a road at Littleworth Common.

Turn left onto this road and follow it for nearly $\frac{1}{2}$ mile, ignoring two turnings to the right and passing Dropmore's Victorian church and the Jolly Woodman. At a right-hand bend in a dip in the road, fork left up a track. In a few yards turn left onto a track towards Hicknaham Farm. By the farm, turn right along a rough lane, forking left of a wood. Just past a belt of trees on the left, turn left over a stile by a gate and follow a fence across the field. On reaching a hedge, turn right over a stile and follow the hedge until you reach a road called Green Common Lane. Go straight on along this road, soon bearing left. Just after this bend, by a holly tree, turn right and follow a line of fence posts across a field to a stile in the corner of a wood. Follow an obvious path through the wood to another stile. Having crossed this, follow the edge of the wood, crossing a stile at the first field boundary, a double set of wooden rails at the second and a stile at the third. Shortly after this, a stile to the right leads you into the wood and across its corner to another stile out of the wood. You resume following a belt of trees, now concealing Hall Barn Park.

At the far side of the field, turn sharp left and double back across the field, heading for the corner of a hedge and a line of trees. Make for the right-hand end of a clump of trees ahead and, turning slightly left here, aim for the end of a hedge. Follow the left-hand side of this hedge to a stile into a disused lane. Follow the lane for $\frac{1}{3}$ mile, finally passing Over's Farm and emerging into a narrow road. Cross the road and a stile and go diagonally across a field to a stile onto another road left of the centre of a wood ahead. Here cross the road and take a path into the wood, ignoring branching paths, until reaching a T-junction with a crossing path. Turn left here and at the far end of a 'tunnel' of holly, turn right onto a path. After 25 yards, by a holly bush, fork left onto another path and follow this downhill, ignoring two crossing tracks, to a stile into a field. Bear half left across the field to a stile. Cross the stile and continue straight on across the next field, heading towards a distant factory chimney, to a stile leading onto Windsor Hill. From here you retrace your steps to Wooburn Green.

Walk 28   Burnham Beeches

4¾ miles (7.5 km)

Start: East Burnham Common; O S map ref. 956851

Burnham Beeches, which serve as a 'green lung' and wooded playground for London, its western suburbs and the nearby dormitory towns and villages, represent a milestone in British conservation history. Their purchase in 1878 by the Corporation of the City of London, together with the purchase of Epping Forest, shows public authority in Victorian England becoming aware of the need to conserve the countryside and taking active steps to fulfil this requirement. Burnham Beeches also have a unique characteristic which is of interest to the countryman as well as the urban dweller: the gnarled ancient beeches which, in some cases, may be up to a thousand years old. They have survived this long because, until 1820, they were regularly pollarded for firewood and for making charcoal. It is this treatment which has caused their fantastic shapes. The end result is that the Beeches resemble primeval forests and contrast sharply with modern managed woodlands. If the peak visiting periods (i.e. Summer weekends) are avoided, this walk can be both interesting and as enjoyable as any in the Chilterns, but walkers are urged to follow the description carefully as these woods are a maze of paths and it is easy to get lost.

The main parking area of Burnham Beeches and the start of the walk, East Burnham Common, may be reached by leaving the M4 at Junction 6 (Slough Central) and following the A355 towards Beaconsfield for 3¾ miles; or leaving the M40 at Junction 2 (Beaconsfield) and following the A355 towards Slough for 2¾ miles to Farnham Royal Shopping Parade, where a side road is signposted to Burnham Beeches. Turn into this road and after crossing a crossroads, the car park is reached.

Starting at a point between the first and second speed humps in the road along which the parking area is situated, (as seen approaching from Farnham Royal) turn right along the edge of the grass area to the right. On entering the woods an obvious path leads you downhill to a culvert over a stream. Cross this and carry straight on uphill, crossing a stony track and then walking parallel with a road to the right, until joining it just before the intriguingly named hamlet of Egypt (thought to derive from its once being frequented by gypsies).

Continue straight on along the road through Egypt for ⅓ mile. Shortly after the houses on the right are replaced by woodland, turn left over a stile beside a white gate and follow a concrete drive between houses, until entering woodland. At the end of the concrete drive, go

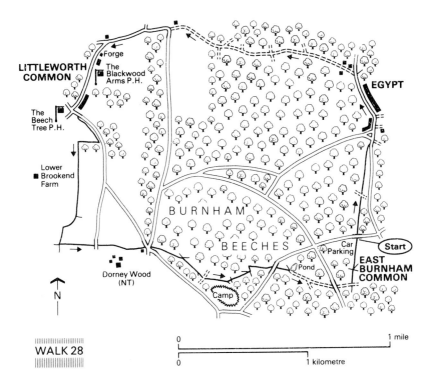

0   1 mile

0   1 kilometre

straight on along a wide woodland track, bearing slightly left where it forks. Continue straight on until you emerge at the edge of the wood. Here bear half left, then half right, ignoring a right-hand, then a left-hand branch. Leave the wood by a stile next to two gates. Continue straight on beside a hedge to another stile by two gates. Cross this and follow a rough lane to the bend in a road. Go straight on along this road for ⅓ mile, ignoring a right-hand turn to Beaconsfield. Opposite a cottage at the beginning of Littleworth Common turn left into Common Lane and follow this for a further ⅓ mile, passing an old village forge with a double stable-type door, passing the Blackwood Arms and going through a wood, until reaching the Beech Tree crossroads.

Turn left here and, after a few yards, turn right over a stile. Now turn left along the hedge and follow the perimeter of the field around three sides, until reaching a corner by some large oaks. Turn left here and follow the left-hand hedge, ignoring a stile to the left in the second field. At the end of the second field, turn left between two holly bushes to a stile at the end of the third field. Cross some rails to the left of this stile and turn left across a field to a stile and gate into a road. Cross the road and continue straight on beside a right-hand hedge. Halfway across the field, Dorneywood House, previously obscured by outbuildings, becomes visible to the right. This house of comparatively modern origin was given to the National Trust as the official residence for a government minister.

At the end of this field, cross a stile re-entering Burnham Beeches. Now cross a road junction to a path commencing between a holly tree and a Corporation of London noticeboard. Continue straight on along this path, passing a large clearing and some gorse bushes to the right. Then, by a hollybush, turn right onto an obvious path and follow this downhill. Just past a gnarled beech tree, ignore two branching paths to the right and on reaching a wide crossing track called Victoria Drive, continue straight on along a path, climbing past a horserail. The unusual appearance of the ground to the right is caused by an ancient earthwork. Near the top of a rise, ignore a fork to the right and a crossing path and continue straight on, dropping into a hollow, where the path merges with another from the left and reaches a T-junction. Turn left here onto a path which shortly bears left by a small clearing. On reaching a larger clearing, turn right and follow an ill-defined path along a glade, until reaching a boundary ridge. Bear half left along this ridge, until the near side becomes covered with bushes, then cross it and go straight out to a road.

Cross this road and bear half left through the trees, soon joining a path which passes to the right of a large lily pond. By the pond, this path becomes a wide track. Follow it uphill and where it forks, go left. Cross a road on the left-hand side of a clearing and continue straight on along another track. Ignore a branching path to the right, then turn left onto a crossing path. After crossing a stream, take the left-centre option at a four-way fork. Soon you emerge onto East Burnham Common on the far side of which is your point of departure.

Walk 29   Fulmer

6¾ miles (10.5 km)

Start: Fulmer Church; O S map ref. 999857
Several parts of the walk tend to be swampy, even in dry weather

---

Fulmer, the name of which is a contraction of the medieval
'Fouwelemere' meaning 'lake of birds', is built in a marshy location
near the source of the Alder Bourne, where a lake and extensive
marshes, populated by ducks and swans, still exist. Despite its
proximity to Greater London, the village of Fulmer, unlike most of its
neighbours, has been allowed to survive largely unaltered with its
attractive seventeenth-century church, eighteenth-century pub, a few
cottages and two interesting manor houses nearby. The church,
unusual for the Chilterns in being built of brick, was built by Sir Mar-
maduke Darrell in 1610 and contains a monument to him. Fulmer
Place, on the Gerrards Cross road, is an eighteenth-century house,
built on the site of Darrell's old manor house; and Fulmer Hall, visible
from Hay Lane was built in 1833.

The walk passes Fulmer Hall and the source of the Alder Bourne as
well as taking in the delightful, unspoilt village of Hedgerley and
some fine heavily wooded landscape in between.

Fulmer, 1½ miles south of Gerrards Cross, may be reached from
Uxbridge or the Denham roundabout by taking the A40 to the French
Horn junction at Gerrards Cross, then turning left onto the road to
Fulmer. At Fulmer, turn right by the church into Hay Lane, a cul-de-
sac, where parking space is available.

Starting from Fulmer church, cross the main road into Hay Lane
and follow it to its end, passing Fulmer Hall on the hillside to the left.
At the end of the lane, fork half right through the frame of an old
kissing-gate and follow an obvious path inside the edge of the wood
near the source of the Alder Bourne. Where the path forks go straight
on over a stile, leaving the wood, and follow the outside edge of the
wood to another stile. (Beware; this field is marshy!). Cross this stile
and then continue across the field on a line parallel to the right-hand
hedge. On reaching another hedge, go through a gap and step over a
slack barbed-wire fence, then bear half right across the next field to a
stile and gate to the right of a small shed. Cross the stile and a farm
track, bearing slightly left, and continue over a second stile onto a
fenced path. This leads out to the B416 on the outskirts of Gerrards
Cross.

Turn right onto this road, then, before reaching the M40 bridge,
turn left into Mount Hill Lane. Cross a stile by a white gate, where the

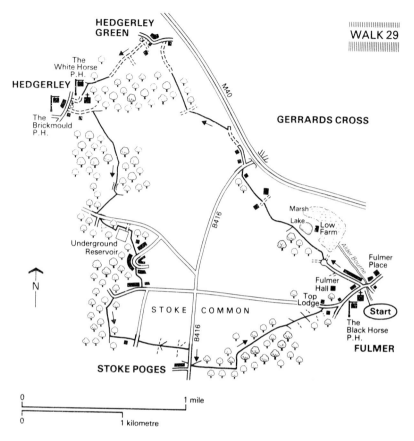

HEDGERLEY
GREEN

The
White Horse
P.H.

HEDGERLEY

The
Brickmould
P.H.

GERRARDS CROSS

Marsh
Lake

Low
Farm

Underground
Reservoir

Fulmer
Place

Fulmer
Hall

Top
Lodge

Start

STOKE   COMMON

The
Black Horse
P.H.

FULMER

STOKE POGES

N

M40

B416

B416

Alder Bourne

0   1 mile

0   1 kilometre

lane ceases to be a public road, and follow its rough continuation to its
end. Here turn left over a stile by a gate and follow the left-hand hedge
through a field, until you reach a stile and gate on a track from the
tunnel under the motorway. Cross the stile and then turn right,
following the right-hand hedge uphill to a stile into a wood. Inside the
wood, continue straight on along an obvious path. On leaving the
wood, the path becomes a narrow hedged lane. Follow this out to a
road at Hedgerley Green. Turn left into the road, bending right past
Manor Farm, then turn left onto a driveway between two ponds. Continue straight on along this, disregarding two branching tracks to the
left. Gradually the wide track narrows and becomes a path. Follow its
obvious course through a wood, ignoring a branching path to the right
where the path bears left. A few yards further on, the path emerges
from the wood by Hedgerley Church.

This picturesque church was only built in 1852 to replace another
nearby which was demolished in the same year. It contains a number

of relics from the earlier building, including a piece of seventeenth-century velvet, reputed to be the remains of a cloak given to the church by King Charles II as an altar cloth.

Turn right down the church drive to the village street, and here turn left. Just past the pond on the left, turn left into a lane and follow this to a gate and stile at its end. Cross the stile and bear half right across a field, heading for a stile into a wood just right of the far corner of the field. Inside the wood, follow an obvious path climbing through it to a stile into the corner of a field. Cross the stile and follow the outside edge of the wood straight on to a footbridge and two stiles. Having crossed these, continue to follow the outside edge of the wood round a corner to a further stile. Do not cross this, but turn sharp right, crossing the field diagonally to a stile near a large Scots pine leading onto a road.

Turn left along the road and at a road junction, fork half right onto a footpath into a wood. Follow this path, ignoring branching paths to the right, to the fence surrounding an underground reservoir. Turn left here and follow the fence until you cross the entrance drive to the reservoir. Here turn right, still following the fence, until a fenced path leads you away from it and eventually out to a road. Turn right along the road. Just past a house called Footsteps, turn right onto a fenced path through some woodland to another road. Here turn right again and follow the road to a sharp right-hand bend. Turn left onto an obvious bridleway along the inside edge of a wood. After $\frac{1}{4}$ mile, turn left over some decrepit iron railings. Follow the right-hand fence across a field to some rails leading to a road. Cross the road and continue straight on along a fenced path. Where this opens out onto Stoke Common, disregard all branching paths and go straight on, bearing right at a fork halfway across the common and emerging by a stile at the B416.

Turn right, and just past a bus stop turn left into a bridleway onto the common, taking the right-hand track which follows the boundary ditch marking the edge of the common. Follow this ditch for $\frac{3}{4}$ mile, turning sharp left after $\frac{1}{4}$ mile. In places, it may be necessary to leave the ditch for a few yards to circumvent swampy areas, but it should be kept in view to prevent your getting lost. Where the ditch turns right by a hollybush, fork left away from it and follow a path straight on across the common, ignoring all branching and crossing tracks. Eventually you emerge at a road opposite Top Lodge. Turn right onto this road and left at a junction back into Fulmer.

Walk 30   Black Park

5 miles (8 km)

Start: Black Park Lake car park; O S map ref. 005832

Black Park and its neighbour on the other side of the A412, Langley
Park, were purchased jointly by Bucks County Council, the former
Eton RDC and Slough Borough Council in 1944, to preserve this
remarkably beautiful and rural tract of countryside between Slough
and Uxbridge from the threat of urban development. One result of
this is that the area is now often overpopulated with visitors but at
quiet times its beauty can still be appreciated. Black Park, so called
because of its afforestation with firs, has an attractive lake which is
reminiscent of those of the Black Forest or the forest lakes of
Scandinavia. Langley Park boasts an eighteenth-century mansion,
built by the Marlborough family as a residence closer to London than
Blenheim Palace, a rhododendron garden and a wealth of fine trees,
as well as its own lake. The walk takes in both these parks as well as
land to the west.

Black Park, $2\frac{1}{2}$ miles northeast of Slough, may be reached from the
A40 at Denham roundabout by taking the A412 towards Slough for $3\frac{1}{2}$
miles and then turning right onto a road to Stoke Poges and Wexham
Street, reaching the large car park on the right in $\frac{1}{2}$ mile. As the car
park is closed at night, walkers arriving late in the day should check
the time of closing. If in doubt, good laybys also exist a little further
along the road.

Starting from the car park near Black Park Lake, head southwards
to the shore of the lake and follow the lakeside path anti-clockwise
around its south-western end. Just past the refreshment kiosk in the
trees to the right, fork half right onto a wide path into the woods.
Follow this path straight on for $\frac{1}{2}$ mile, disregarding all crossing
tracks, until you reach the A412 dual-carriageway road virtually
opposite Billet Lane. Cross this busy road carefully and follow Billet
Lane straight on for over $\frac{1}{4}$ mile. Just before the first right-hand bend,
turn right between some railings into Langley Park. (The next section
of the walk uses a permissive path through council-owned parkland.
In the unlikely event of it being closed for any reason, an alternative
route on public rights of way is shown on the map.) Pass a
rhododendron garden to the right and the car park to your left, then
take a path parallel to Billet Lane for $\frac{1}{3}$ mile, until you reach a stony
crossing track. Cross this and follow an obvious winding path straight
on, then bear left to a stile, where a public right of way is rejoined.

Cross this stile and follow a wide fenced path between an orchard
and open parkland. At the far end of this section, cross the right-hand

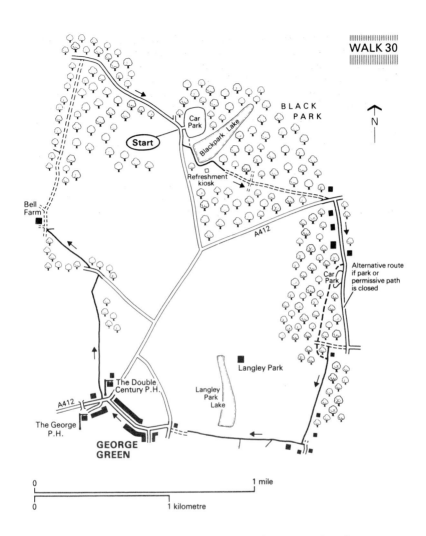

of two stiles, then follow a fenced path straight on, crossing three more stiles, until you reach a crossing fenced path. Turn right onto this and follow it straight on, soon passing through a kissing-gate, for over $\frac{1}{2}$ mile. After $\frac{1}{4}$ mile, Langley Park House can be seen to the right some distance away. At the far side of the park, go through another kissing-gate into a lane and follow it straight on to a road junction. Here go straight on, wiggling slightly right into George Green Road. Follow this through George Green to the A412.

Turn left along the A412 to a pedestrian flyover near the George. Cross this flyover and retrace your steps on the other side of the road to a stile just before the Double Century. Turn left here over this and a second stile. Continue straight on across two fields and over two more stiles. Then, heading left of a distant copse, go straight on across a larger field to a stile and gate. Here bear slightly left across the next field to a stile in some wooden rails. Having crossed this, follow a right-hand hedge to a stile into a road. Turn left along this road. After a few yards, fork right onto a path through a belt of trees to a stile. Cross this and bear half left across a field, heading for distant farm buildings at Bell Farm. Eventually you emerge by way of a stile and gate into a lane called Gallions Lane by the farm. Here turn right along this lane and after 150 yards, where the main vehicular track bears left into a field, bear right and continue to follow Gallions Lane, now a hedged bridleway, for $\frac{3}{4}$ mile to a road. Turn right and follow the road straight on for $\frac{1}{2}$ mile to the point of departure.